Biblical
MOURNING

Register This New Book

Benefits of Registering*

- ✓ FREE **replacements** of lost or damaged books
- ✓ FREE **audiobook** – *Pilgrim's Progress*, audiobook edition
- ✓ FREE information about new titles and other **freebies**

www.anekopress.com/new-book-registration

*See our website for requirements and limitations.

Biblical
MOURNING

Or, A Token for Mourners

*Encouragement for Those
Who Lost Loved Ones*

JOHN FLAVEL

We love hearing from our readers. Please contact us at www.anekopress.com/questions-comments with any questions, comments, or suggestions.

Biblical Mourning - Or, A Token for Mourners
© 2022 by Aneko Press
First edition 1813.
Revisions copyright 2022.

Please do not reproduce, store in a retrieval system, or transmit in any form or by any means – electronic, mechanical, photocopying, recording, or otherwise, without written permission from the publisher. Please contact us via www.AnekoPress.com for reprint and translation permissions.

Scripture quotations from The Authorized (King James) Version. Rights in the Authorized Version in the United Kingdom are vested in the Crown. Reproduced by permission of the Crown's patentee, Cambridge University Press.

Cover Designer: Jonathan Lewis
Editors: Charlene Miskimen and Ruth Clark

Aneko Press
www.anekopress.com
Aneko Press, Life Sentence Publishing, and our logos are trademarks of
Life Sentence Publishing, Inc.
203 E. Birch Street
P.O. Box 652
Abbotsford, WI 54405

RELIGION / Christian Living / Death, Grief, Bereavement
Paperback ISBN: 978-1-62245-748-9
eBook ISBN: 978-1-62245-749-6
10 9 8 7 6 5 4 3 2 1
Available where books are sold

Contents

Introduction vii

Ch. 1 Looking to Christ... 1

Ch. 2 Signs of Excessive Sorrow 13

Ch. 3 God's Sovereignty... 33

Ch. 4 Excuses 91

Ch. 5 The Cure 111

John Flavel – A Brief Biography 119

Other Similar Titles 125

Introduction

Dear Friends,

Because we have been tied together by nature and grace and have over the years spent so many delightful times together that have linked and glued our emotions, I cannot help but feel tender sympathy with you because of all your troubles and say of every affliction that you suffer, "Half is mine." I find it is with our emotions as with the strings of musical instruments exactly set at the same height: if one is touched, the other trembles though it is at some distance.

Our emotions are one, and so in a great measure, our afflictions have been also. You cannot forget that it was just recently that the Almighty visited my home with the rod and, in one year, cut off from it the root and the branch – the tender mother and the only son. I have felt the effects of those blows, or rather of my own unchecked passions, and you and others have heard. I was as a bull unaccustomed to the yoke. Yes, I may say with them, *Remembering mine affliction and my misery, the wormwood and the gall. My soul hath them still in remembrance, and is humbled in me* (Lamentations 3:19-20).

I will say that I never felt my heart discontentedly

rising and swelling against God; no, I could still justify him even when I felt the most pain from his hand. If he had plunged me into a sea of sorrow, I could say in all that sea of sorrow that there is not a drop of injustice. It was my emotions and passions – feverish, exaggerated, and unchecked – that made such sad impressions on my body and put me into such bad moods that even my remaining comforts were bitter to me.

It was my earnest desire, as soon as I had the opportunity and the strength, to make the great journey to visit you so that, if the Lord had pleased, I might both refresh and be refreshed by you after all my sad and cheerless days. And you cannot imagine what contentment and pleasure I projected in that visit, but it proved to us, as all other comforts of the same kind ordinarily do, more in expectation than in fruition, for how soon after our joyful meeting and embraces did the Lord overcast and darken our day by sending death into your home to take away the desire of your eyes with one stroke! Death cropped off that sweet and only bud from which we promised ourselves so much comfort.

But no more of that. I fear I have gone too far already. It is not my purpose to exasperate your troubles, but to heal them. For that purpose, I have sent you these papers that I hope may be of use both to you and many others in your condition, since they are the product of my own troubles. These are not things that I have recommended to you from another hand, but things that I have, in some measure, proved and tasted in my own trials.

I have only a few things I desire for you and from you, and then I will close.

First, I desire that you will not be too hasty to remove the yoke that God has put on your neck. Remember, when your child was in the womb, neither of you desired that it should be delivered until God's fully appointed time had come. Now that you are filled with sorrow for his death, do not desire to be delivered from your sorrows one moment before God's time. Let patience have its perfect work so that comfort, which comes in God's way and season, may remain and do you good.

Second, even though you and your afflictions had a sad meeting, I desire that you and they may have a comfortable parting. If they do the work in your hearts that God sent them for, I have no doubt you will give them a fair testimony when they leave. What you endured with fear, you will dismiss with praise. How sweet it is, when God is loosing his hands, to hear the afflicted soul say, "It is good for me that I have been afflicted!"

Third, I heartily wish that these searching afflictions may make the most satisfying discoveries. May you now see more of the evil of sin, the vanity of the creature, and the fullness of Christ. Afflictions are searchers and cause the soul to search and test its way (Lamentations 3). *Blessed is the man whom thou chastenest, O* LORD, *and teachest him out of thy law* (Psalm 94:12). Many times, there are unseen causes of our troubles, and now you have the advantage of sifting out the seeds from which they come.

Fourth, I wish that all the love and delight you gave to your little one may now be placed, to your greater advantage, on Jesus Christ. The stream of your love and affection for him can be much stronger as there are now fewer channels for it to be divided into. If the jealousy of the Lord removed what took too much of your heart from him, then deliver it all up to him and say, "Lord, take my whole heart for yourself."

Fifth, I desire that you may be strengthened with all might to all patience in your inner being (Ephesians 3:16), and that the peace of God may keep your hearts and minds (Philippians 4:7). Labor to bring your hearts to a meek submission to the rod of your Father. Our earthly fathers corrected us, and we gave them reverence. Should we not be in even more subjection to the Father of spirits? It is not good for a child to contest and fight with his father. Someone wisely observed that the soul grows wise by sitting still and quiet under the rod, and the author of Hebrews calls those fruits that the saints gather from their sanctified afflictions *the peaceable fruit of righteousness* (Hebrews 12:11).

Last, my heart's desire and prayer to God for you is that you may die daily to all visible pleasures, and that by these frequent encounters with death in your family, you may be prepared for your own deaths when they come.

O friends! How many graves have you and I seen dug for our dear relatives? How often has death come up into your windows and summoned the delight of your eyes? In just a little while, we will go to them. We and they are separated only by short intervals of time.

Our dear parents are gone, our lovely and desirable children are gone, our close relatives that were as our own souls are gone. All these warning knocks at our doors teach us that we must prepare to follow shortly after them.

Oh, I hope that these things make our own death both easier and more familiar to us! The more often death visits us, the better we will be acquainted with it, and the more of our loved ones it takes before us, the fewer snares or entanglements remain for us when our own turn comes.

My dear friends, I beg you for religion's sake, for your own sake, and for my sake, whose comfort is, in great part, bound up in your success and welfare, to believingly apply these Scripture consolations and directions that I have gathered for your use. May the God of all consolation be with you.

Your most endeared brother,
John Flavel

Chapter 1

Looking to Christ

Now when he came nigh to the gate of the city, behold, there was a dead man carried out, the only son of his mother, and she was a widow: and much people of the city was with her. And when the Lord saw her, he had compassion on her, and said unto her, Weep not. (Luke 7:12-13)

To be above feelings and emotions is a condition equal to the angels. To be in a state of sorrow without the sense of sorrow is a disposition beneath the beasts. But to correctly regulate our sorrows and bind our passions under suffering is the wisdom, duty, and excellency of a Christian.

Those who are without natural affections are deservedly ranked among the worst of heathens, and those who are able to properly manage them deserve to be numbered with the best of Christians. When we are sanctified, we put on the divine nature, but until we are glorified, we still bear the infirmities of our human nature.

As long as we are within the reach of troubles, we are in danger of sin and ought not to be without the fear of sin. It is as hard for us to escape sin while in adversity as when we are lulled by prosperity.

Most people are likely to transgress the bounds of both reason and religion under sharp affliction. So it is with this woman. Christ puts a stop to her excessive sorrow: *When the Lord saw her, he had compassion on her, and said unto her, Weep not.*

When the Lord saw the moaning and weeping of this distressed mother, he was moved in tender compassion and had more pity in his heart for her than could be in her heart for her dear and only son.

In these words, we will consider both the condition of the woman and the counsel of Christ concerning her condition.

The Condition of the Woman

She appears to be very heartbroken and distressed. Her groans and tears moved and melted the very heart of Christ to hear and see them: *When [he] saw her, he had compassion on her.*

We can see what a sad time this was for her in Luke's clear remarks: *Now when he [Christ] came nigh to the gate of the city, behold, there was a dead man carried out, the only son of his mother, and she was a widow: and much people of the city was with her.* In this one verse, Luke notes several heart-piercing circumstances of this affliction.

It was the death of a son. To bury a child, any child, tears the heart of a tender parent; for what are children, but the parent multiplied? A child is a part of the parent made up in another skin. But to lay a son in the grave, a son who continues the name and supports the family – this was always considered a very great affliction.

This son was not carried from the cradle to the coffin nor stripped out of his baby clothes to be wrapped in his grave clothes. If he had died in his infancy before he had returned her affection or raised expectations, the affliction might not have been so sharp and cutting as it was. Death struck the son in the flower and prime of his time. He was a man, a young man. Christ says, *Young man, I say unto thee, Arise* (Luke 7:14). He was now at that age that made him capable of giving to his mother all the comfort that had been the expectation and hope of many years, and the reward and fruit of many cares and labors. Now, when the feelings and attachments were greatest and her hopes highest, in the flower of his age, he was cut off.

In the same way, Basil mourned the death of his son: "I once had a son, who was a young man, my only successor, the solace of my age, the glory of his kind, the prop of my family, and had arrived at the endearing age. Then he was snatched away from me by death. I heard his lovely voice just a little before he died, and he recently had been a pleasant sight to his parent."[1]

Reader, if this has happened to you, as it has to me, I do not need to say any more to convince you that it was a sorrowful state indeed in which Christ met this tender mother.

He was not only a son but also an only son. He was *the only son of his mother,* the one in whom all her hopes and comforts were bound. All her affections were contracted into this one object. If we were to have ever so many children, we would not know which of them to spare. If they stood like olive plants around our tables, it would grieve us to see the least twig among them broken down. But still, the death of one out of many is more tolerable than all in one.

For this reason, it is noted in Scripture as the greatest of earthly sorrows: *O daughter of my people, gird thee with sackcloth, and wallow thyself in ashes: make thee mourning, as for an only son, most bitter lamentation: for the spoiler shall suddenly come upon us* (Jeremiah 6:26). Yes, so deep and penetrating is this grief that the Holy Spirit borrows it to express the deepest spiritual troubles: *They shall mourn for him [Christ], as one mourneth for his only son* (Zechariah 12:10).

To heighten the affliction, the author further adds, *And she was a widow.* The staff of her old age on which

---

[1] Basil (330–379) was an early church theologian.

she leaned was broken. She now had no one left to comfort or assist her in her helpless, comfortless state of widowhood. It was a condition not only void of comfort but also exposed to oppression and contempt.

Being a widow, the whole burden lay on her alone. She did not have a husband to comfort her as Elkanah did Hannah: *Why weepest thou? and why eatest thou not? and why is thy heart grieved? am not I better to thee than ten sons?* (1 Samuel 1:8). This would have been a great relief, but her husband was dead as well as her son. They were both gone, and she was the only one left to lament the loss of those comforts she once had. Her calamities did not come alone, but one after another. This revived and aggravated the former. This was her case and condition when the Lord met her.

The Counsel That Christ Gave Her

In the words of Christ's relieving and supporting counsel, let us consider the occasion for it, the motive, and the counsel itself. *And when the Lord saw her, he had compassion on her, and said unto her, Weep not.*

The occasion of Christ's counsel was his seeing the widow. This meeting at the gate of the city, however accidental it seems, was without doubt providentially suited to the work intended to be done. The eye of his omniscience foresaw her, and this meeting was designed by him as an occasion for him to work this miracle on the young man.

Christ has an eager eye to discern poor, mourning,

and inconsolable creatures. Though he is now in heaven and out of our sight, he sees us, and his eye, which sees all our troubles, still affects his heart and moves him to be compassionate towards us.

The motive stirring him to give this comforting counsel to her was his own compassion. She neither expected nor asked for it from him, but the Lord was so full of tender pity toward her that he goes before her with unexpected consolation. Christ had more compassion for her than she did for her son. He bore our infirmities, natural as well as moral ones, in the days of his flesh, and though he is now exalted to the highest glory, he is still as merciful as ever and just as likely to be touched with the feeling of our miseries (Matthew 8:17; Hebrews 4:15).

The counsel itself was to *Weep not.* Christ, who was anointed to the office of Comforter to those who mourn, is here fulfilling that role (Isaiah 61:1-3). Yet the words are not an absolute prohibition of tears and sorrow; he does not condemn all mourning as sinful or all expressions of grief for dead relatives as unfitting. No, Christ does not want his people mindless and without feeling; he only prohibits the excesses of our sorrows for the dead. We should not mourn for the dead as the heathen do. They sorrow without end because they have no hope. They are ignorant of the grand relief that the gospel reveals.

The resurrection of her son from the dead is the ground on which Christ builds her consolation and relief. He can tell her to stop crying because he intended to soon remove the cause of her tears by restoring her son to life.

There is something extraordinary and peculiar in this case because very few, if any, who carry their dead children to the grave may expect them to be raised from the dead immediately by a special resurrection as this woman did. Those who lose their loved ones now should not expect this because the occasion and reason for such miraculous, special resurrections have been removed by a sufficient and full evidence and confirmation of Christ's divine power and Godhead. But those who do now bury their relatives, if they died in Christ, have as good a reason to moderate their passions as this mourner had. They just as truly come within the reach and bounds of his comfortable and supporting counsel, *Weep not,* as she did. What more comfort or support can a resurrection from the dead give us now than as an illustration and a pledge of the general resurrection? The returning of the soul to its body to live a physical life again in this world of sin and sorrow, only to soon undergo the agonies and pains of death again, is not in itself a benefit that affords much comfort to the person raised or to his relatives. It is no advantage to the person raised, for it returns him from rest to trouble, from the harbor back again into the ocean.

Many dying saints are troubled to hear of the likelihood of their recovering when they have gotten so near to heaven. A godly minister of England who had been close to death but then returned said, "I am like a sheep driven out of the storm almost to the fold and then driven back into the storm again. I am like a weary traveler that has neared his home but then must go back to fetch something he had forgotten, or an apprentice whose commitment time has almost expired but then must begin a new term."

But to actually die and then return from the dead has even less advantage than to return only from the brink of the grave, for the sick have not yet felt the agonies and last struggles and pangs of death. The dead have felt them once and now must feel them again. They must die twice before they can be happy once. Besides, during the little time they spend on earth between their first and second death, there is a perfect amnesia and unawareness of all that they saw or enjoyed in their state of separation. It is necessary both for them and others that it should be so. For themselves it is necessary so that they may be content to live and endure the time of separation from that blessed and indescribable state quietly and patiently. For others, it is so that they may live by faith, not by sense, and build on divine authority and report rather than human. If people were resurrected now, they would have their agonies and pangs doubled, but their lives would not be sweetened by a sense of happiness that returns and remains with them; therefore, it is not an advantage to them.

And as for their relatives, though it might be some

comfort to receive them again from the dead, the thought that they are returned back to this stormy sea to endure new sorrows and troubles from which they had just been freed, and that in a short time they must part with them again and so feel the double sorrows of a parting pull that others feel just once, makes an individual resurrection not the comfort we might at first imagine it to be.

What remains is that the ground of all solid comfort and relief against the death of our relatives lies in the general and last resurrection. What is in an individual resurrection is only an illustration or evidence of the general one. There the apostle Paul places our relief. At the Lord's coming, we will see and enjoy them again (1 Thessalonians 4:17). Certainly this is better than if we, like this mother in the text, have our dead raised to us now as she did her son. If we do not think so, it is because our hearts are carnal and measure things by time and sense rather than by faith and eternity.

We have seen the counsel to the woman and the basis for the counsel that, for the most part and with very little difference, all other Christian mourners share. And we have also seen that there was much sorrow and many magnifications of sorrow. A son, an only son, is carried to the grave, yet Christ commands the melancholy woman not to mourn. So, we note that Christians ought to moderate their sorrows for their dead loved ones, no matter how many afflictions and aggravating circumstances come together in their deaths.

It is as common for people, good people, to go to extremes in their sorrow for their dead relatives as it is for them to go to excess in their love and delights of living relatives. They both are hard to confine, as they say of waters, within their bounds. Therefore, it is grave advice that the apostle Paul delivers: *But this I say, brethren, the time is short: it remaineth, that both they that have wives be as though they had none; and they that weep, as though they wept not; and they that rejoice, as though they rejoiced not* (1 Corinthians 7:29-30).

It is as if he had said the world is near its end. God has contracted the sails of man's life; he has shortened their years. We have only a point of time to live, and shortly it will be past the time to choose whether we had wives or not, children or not. All these are time-eaten things, and before the expected fruit of these comforts is ripe, we ourselves may be rotten. Therefore, it is wise to look on things that soon will not be as if they already were not, and to behave ourselves in the loss of these physical joys as the natural man behaves himself in the use of spiritual practices. He hears as if he did not hear, and we should weep as if we did not weep. Their feelings are sometimes moved a little by spiritual things, but they never take them to heart so as to be brokenhearted for the sin they hear of or deeply affected by the glory revealed. We also should feel the stroke of God on our dear relatives, but we must weep as if we did not weep. That is, we must keep appropriate boundaries and moderation in our sorrow and not be too deeply concerned for these dying, short-lived things.

It is for this purpose that the author of Hebrews exhorts, *My son, despise not thou the chastening of the Lord, nor faint when thou art rebuked of him* (Hebrews 12:5). Despising and fainting are two extremes. To despise the Lord's chastening is to say when he is correcting us, "I do not care. Let God take it all if he will. If my estate must go, let it go. If my children die, let them die." God cannot bear that we would treat it all so lightly.

The other extreme is fainting. Fainting under God's rod would be when goods are taken away, the heart goes also, and when children die, the spirit of the parent also dies. Seneca, the Roman statesman and philosopher, said, "You lament your deceased friend, but I would not have you grieve beyond what is fit. I dare not require you to not grieve at all; tears may be excused if they do not exceed. Let your eyes, therefore, be neither wholly dry nor let them overflow. Weep you may, but wail you must not." People who keep the bridle of moderation on their passions and emotions and still keep possession of themselves, no matter what they lose, will be happy people.

Now, I propose to consider this subject of excessive sorrow in several steps. First, I will help you discover the signs of excessive sorrow, and then I will try to dissuade you from that sin. Next, I will attempt to remove your excuses, and finally, I will propose the cure.

Chapter 2

Signs of Excessive Sorrow

I will give you the signs of excessive sorrow and show you when it exceeds its bounds and becomes sinful, because even true sorrow can be sinful. For the sake of clarity, I will first state what may be allowed for the Christian mourner, and then you will be better able to discern where the excess and sinfulness of your sorrow lies.

First, no matter how much we censure and condemn excessive sorrow, the afflicted persons must be allowed an aware and tender sense of the Lord's afflicting hand on them. It is no virtue to bear what we do not feel, and it would be most unfitting to not tremble when God is striking.

Talking about Miriam, the Lord said to Moses, *If her father had but spit in her face, should she not be ashamed seven days?* (Numbers 12:14). The face is the seat of beauty and honor, but when it is spit on, it is made the site of shame. God says if her own father had spit on her face when she had displeased him, she would have gone away ashamed of such a rebuke and not showed her face for seven days. How much more should she take to heart and be sensible of this rebuke of God, who has filled her face with leprous spots, the signs of his displeasure against her! God will certainly be ashamed of those who are not ashamed when he rebukes them.

It is not magnanimity to make light of God's corrections, it is stupidity. For this, the afflicted are quickly condemned: *Thou hast stricken them, but they have not grieved* (Jeremiah 5:3). When God struck Job's body, his children, and his estate, Job got up, tore his clothes, and put dust on his head to show that he was not without feeling and unaffected. Then he blessed the God who afflicted him, showing plainly that he was not rebellious or disobedient.

Second, we must allow mourning and afflicted souls a due and appropriate expression of their grief and sorrow in their complaints both to God and other people. It is much more fitting for Christians to honestly express their troubles than to sullenly smother them. It is perhaps not a sin to complain *to* God, but there is much wickedness in complaining *of* him. Griefs are eased by groans, and the pressures of the heart are relieved by speech. This was how David, who was a man of afflictions, constantly

> It is perhaps not a sin to complain *to* God, but there is much wickedness in complaining *of* him.

lived: *I poured out my complaint before him; I shewed before him my trouble. When my spirit was overwhelmed within me, then thou knewest my path* (Psalm 142:2-3).

To whom should children go besides their father to moan and complain? Where should they expect relief and comfort except from him? Psalm 102 is entitled, *A Prayer of the afflicted, when he is overwhelmed, and poureth out his complaint before the LORD* (AKJV). It would be good if every afflicted soul chose this way to express sorrow. If we complained more to God, he would complain less of us and quickly lessen the matters of our complaint.

Oh, you cannot imagine how moving, how softening, how prevailing it is with God when his poor, burdened, oppressed, and afflicted people, in the day of distress and despondency, when deep calls to deep and one wave drives on another, turn to him and with humility, filial confidence, and faith speak to him like this:

"Father, what should I do? My soul is greatly burdened by trouble. I have reached my limit. My vain heart has looked for relief this way and that way, but none comes; every door of comfort is shut against me. You have multiplied my sorrows and brought new witnesses against me (Job 10:17). You have removed comfort from my body and peace from my soul. There are sharp afflictions without and bitter reflections within. O Lord, I am oppressed. Turn to me. Earthly fathers pity their distressed children when they complain to them. O Lord, whose compassion as far exceeds human compassion as the sea exceeds a drop, will you not pity me as well? O my Father! Pity me, support me, deliver me!"

How acceptable this is to God and how advantageous to the soul!

We may also make our complaint to men. Job did: *Have pity upon me, have pity upon me, O ye my friends; for the hand of God hath touched me* (Job 19:21). It is a mercy if we have friends that are wise, faithful, and experienced; they are born for such a time as this (Proverbs 17:17). But no matter how good our friends may be, they cannot pity as God can, nor can they relieve and support as well as he can. Often we may say with Job, *As for me, is my complaint to man? and if it were so, why should not my spirit be troubled?* (Job 21:4). There is not a great advantage to making these complaints. I may burden the heart of my friend, but it does little to ease my own. Yet opening your heart to an experienced, tender Christian is some relief, and their prayer for you is even more. In this kind of sorrow, you are safe. There is no danger.

Third, the afflicted people may ordinarily accuse, judge, and condemn themselves for being the cause of their own troubles. They may lawfully be discontented and angry with themselves for their own foolishness when the iniquity of their heels encompasses them (Psalm 49:5). And truly it is rare that gracious people do not see the need of the rod of great affliction before they feel it.

Has God struck your child or friend? Did you not foresee some sharp trial coming? Did your indulgent, complacent, and carnal temper need a scourge to waken, revive, and purge you? If you did not see it coming, you must now search and examine yourselves. The church, in her affliction, resolved, *Let us search and try our ways* (Lamentations 3:40). When God is striking, we should be searching. The consequences of our sins will certainly find us if we do not seek to discover our sins. Yes, in the day of affliction, a gracious soul is inquisitive only about what brought on its troubles. *Shew me wherefore thou contendest with me* (Job 10:2). "Lord, what specific sin is this rod sent to rebuke? What sinful neglect does it come to humble me for? Oh, reveal it to me now and help me recover from it."

> When God is striking, we should be searching.

When they find the root and cause of their troubles, sincere souls will shame themselves for it and give glory to God by humble submission and vindication of the equity and righteousness of God's actions. *I have sinned; what shall I do unto thee, O thou preserver of men?* (Job 7:20). They are not ashamed to freely admit their sin to God and to debase and humble themselves before him because of their folly.

I remember an excellent note that Thomas Brightman has in his commentary on the Song of Solomon. He says, "Holy men, after their hearts are renewed by repentance, are not ashamed to remember and confess their slips and shameful falls to the glory of God. For they consider that the glory that such confessions take from them is not lost; it instead adds to the glory of God." If his glory rises out of our shame, how willing should we be to take this shame upon us? David was not ashamed to acknowledge: *My wounds stink and are corrupt because of my foolishness* (Psalm 38:5). They are wisest who make themselves fools before God.

It is true, God may afflict to accomplish his sovereign purpose or for our trial, but we may always see cause enough in ourselves, and it is safest to charge it to our own foolishness.

Last, the afflicted Christian may, in a humble and submissive manner, earnestly plead with God for the removal of his affliction. When affliction presses us beyond our strength, when it disables us for duty, or when it gives the advantage to temptation, then we may say with David, *Remove thy stroke away from me: I am consumed by the blow of thine hand* (Psalm 39:10). Even our Lord Jesus Christ, in the day of his troubles, poured out his soul with strong cries and many tears, *saying, Father, if thou be willing, remove this cup from me* (Luke 22:42). Oppressed natures desire ease, and even our renewed natures desire freedom from those obstructions and temptations that hinder us in duty or expose us to snares.

These things we are allowed, but they are as far as we may safely go. Let us now consider the signs of sinful sorrow.

1. Sorrow becomes excessive and sinful when our sorrow causes us to slight and despise all our other mercies and joys as small things in comparison with what we have lost. It often happens that the loss of one comfort clouds and darkens all the rest. Our tears for our lost joys so blind our eyes that we cannot see the many other mercies that remain. We take so much notice of what is gone that we take little or no notice of what is left, but this is very sinful because it involves both ignorance and ingratitude, and it is a great provocation.

It is a sin springing from ignorance. If we knew what our sins deserved, we would be amazed that even one pleasure was left rather than that twenty are cut off. Those who know they have forfeited every mercy should be thankful that they enjoy any at all, and patient when they lose some of their comforts.

> If we knew what our sins deserved, we would be amazed that even one pleasure was left rather than that twenty are cut off.

If you knew that God, the Sovereign Lord at whose disposal our comforts come and go, can in the next moment blast all the comforts that remain and send you into hell afterward, you would prize and value the mercies he still indulges you with even more. If you understood the fickle, vanishing nature of the creature – what a flower, what a bubble it is – how thankful you would be to find so many comforts still in your possession!

If you knew that there are thousands as good as you, and even better than you, whose harvest of comfort in this world is but a handful compared to the gleanings of comforts you still enjoy, who in all their lives never had even the comforts and joys that you now overlook – certainly you would not act as you do.

Not only does your attitude display ignorance, but it also demonstrates such vile ingratitude! Are all your remaining mercies worth nothing? You have buried a child or a friend, but you still have a husband, a wife, or other children. Or if not, you have comfortable accommodations for yourselves with health to enjoy them. And if you do not have that, you have the Word of God, a share in Christ and in the covenant, the pardon of sin, and the hope of glory. Yet you mourn and act as if all your mercies, comforts, and hopes, of both worlds, were buried in one grave! Must *Ichabod,* your regret at what is gone, be written on your best mercies because mortality is written on one (1 Samuel 4:21)? Oh, what shameful ingratitude is here!

And friend, behavior such as this is a provocation to the Lord to go on in judgment and completely take away all that remains so that this cannot happen again.

What if God would take notice of how little you regard the many undeserved favors you still have? What if he would say, "Well, if you do not think they are worth owning, I do not think they are worth continuing. Go, Death. There is a husband, a wife, and other children still left. Strike them all. Go, Sickness. Remove the health they have. Go, Losses. Take away all their belongings and wealth. Go, Reproach. Blast their good reputations."

What would you think of this? Those of you who are not in Christ, you are in danger of a far sadder stroke than anything I have mentioned. What if God would say, "Do you not prize my mercy? Have you no value for my goodness and patience towards you? Is it nothing to you that I have spared you so long in your sins and rebellion? Well then, I will stretch out my hand on your life and cut off that thread that has kept you so many years from dropping into hell."

Oh, think what you have done by provoking the Lord through your vile ingratitude! It is a dangerous thing to provoke God when he is already in a way of judgment. And if you are a child of his and so not in danger of this last and worst stroke, know that you still have better mercies to lose than any you have already lost. If God were to cloud your souls with doubts, let Satan loose to torment you, or remove joy and peace from your heart – how soon you would be convinced that the funeral of your dearest friend is but a trifle compared to this.

So whatever God takes, be thankful for what he leaves. Ingratitude was the great sin of Israel in the wilderness. Even though God had delivered them from their cruel servitude in Egypt, miraculously fed them in the desert, and was leading them to a land flowing with milk and honey, as soon as they began to need anything, all these mercies were forgotten and ignored. *Would God that we had died in the land of Egypt!* (Numbers 14:2). *There is nothing at all, beside this manna* (Numbers 11:6). Beware you mourning and afflicted ones. You can see both the sin that is in excessive sorrow and the danger that accompanies it.

2. Our sorrows are also sinful when they so completely engulf our hearts that we do not care or are even unaware of the evils and calamities that are affecting the church and the people of God. Some Christians have such public spirits that the church's troubles swallow up their personal troubles. Philip Melanchthon, Martin Luther's friend and colleague, seemed to take little notice of the death of the child he dearly loved because he was so overwhelmed with the miseries lying on the church. Scripture offers good evidence of the graciousness and unselfishness of Eli's spirit. He was sitting in the gate, anxiously waiting, when the news came that Israel had fled before the Philistines, that his two sons, Hophni and Phinehas, were dead, and that the ark of God was taken. It was at the mention of those words, *the ark of God,* that he understood the issue, sank down, and died (1 Samuel 4:17-18). Those were the words that killed him. If the messenger had stopped at the death of his two sons, it is likely Eli would have been able to bear that burden, but the loss of the ark was more to him than sons or daughters.

But how few such unselfish spirits there are, even among professing Christians, in this selfish generation! We can complain with Paul: *All seek their own, not the things which are Jesus Christ's* (Philippians 2:21). Few people have any great cares or plans that lie outside the bounds of their own private interests. And what we say of cares is as true of sorrows: if a child dies, we are ready to die too, but public calamities do not bother us.

How few allow either their domestic comforts to be swallowed up in the church's troubles or their domestic troubles to be swallowed up by the church's mercies! Now, when we are sorrowing to excess, when we do not care what mercies or miseries lie on others but are completely focused on our own afflictions – this is sinful sorrow and ought to be sorrowed for.

3. Our sorrows become sinful and exorbitant when they distract us from our duties, so that our fellowship with heaven is stopped and interrupted by them. We can sit alone so long musing on a dead creature. Our thoughts flow easily there, but how hard it is to fix them on the living God! When our hearts should be in heaven with our Christ, they are too often in the grave with our dead. Many afflicted souls justly complain that their troubles took away Christ and their sweet communion with him from them and laid the dead child in his place.

> When our hearts should be in heaven with our Christ, they are too often in the grave with our dead.

O poor soul, do not weep any longer for your dead loved ones. Weep instead for your dead heart. Is this how you comply with God's design in afflicting you – to be more a stranger to him than before? Do you think this is the way to your cure and comfort in affliction – to refrain from prayer and turn your back on God?

Perhaps you do not dare to wholly neglect your duty, but your affliction spoils the success and comfort of it. In prayer and meditation, your heart is so wandering, dead, and distracted that you have no relief or comfort from it.

Rouse yourself, Christian. This is not right. The rod will not work kindly while you sin this way. Did your love for God die when your friend died? Is your heart as cold in spirituality as his body is in the grave? Has natural death seized him, and spiritual deadness seized you?

Certainly, you have more reason to lament your dead heart than your dead friend. Divert the stream of your troubles and strive to work yourself out of this temper quickly so that you do not discover through experience that what you mourn for now is just a trifle compared to what you will mourn for if you do not stop. To lose the heavenly warmth and spiritual liveliness of your affections is undoubtedly a far more considerable loss than to lose your devoted wife or the sweetest child that ever a tender parent laid in the grave.

If this is your situation, you have reason to claim first place among the mourners. It is better for you to bury ten sons than to revoke one degree of love or delight in God. God's purpose in striking you was to bring your heart nearer to him by removing that which estranged it. Why, then, are you going against the very design of God in this matter? Must God lose his delight in your fellowship because you have lost yours in the creature? When your troubles accompany you to your prayer closet, they are sinful and excessive troubles.

> When your troubles accompany you to your prayer closet, they are sinful and excessive troubles.

4. You may also conclude your sorrows to be excessive and sinful when they so overload and oppress your bodies that they endanger your lives or render them useless and unfit for service. *The sorrow of the world worketh death* (2 Corinthians 7:10). The sorrow of the world is the sorrow of worldly people, carnal and unredeemed. It is sorrow that is not relieved by any spiritual reasonings or considerations. Sometimes this falls so heavily on the body that the body sinks under the weight and falls victim to diseases that are unable to be fought off or healed in this world. *Heaviness in the heart of man maketh it stoop* (Proverbs 12:25). Even the strongest body stoops under the pressures of the heart.

When it gets into your mind, grief is a moth that will, in a very short time, make the body, no matter how strong and well made, like an old, worn-out, threadbare garment.

Philosophers and physicians generally count sorrow among the chief causes of shortening life. Christ was *a man of sorrows, and acquainted with grief* (Isaiah 53:3), and this, some think, was the reason that he appeared as a man of fifty when he was little more than thirty years old (John 8:57). But his sorrows were of another kind.

Many people's souls are to their bodies as a sharp knife is to a thin sheath that is easily cut through by the knife. When we are absorbed in and focused on our troubles, we are sharpening the knife so that it can cut deeper and quicker. Of all the creatures that God ever made (only the demons excepted), man is the most able and apt to be his own tormentor.

We so unmercifully load and burden our bodies in times of affliction! Not only do we allow sorrow to sap our bodies' strength, but we also deny them relief and necessary refreshment. They must carry the load but are allowed no refreshment. If they can eat the bread of affliction and drink tears, they may feed to the full, but no pleasant bread or quiet sleep is permitted them. Certainly, you would not burden a beast as you do your own bodies. You would pity and relieve a work animal that was groaning and sinking under a heavy burden, but you will not pity or relieve your own bodies. Some men's souls have given such deep wounds to their bodies that they will not enjoy many easy or comfortable days while they dwell in them.

This is very sinful and displeasing to God. He has such tender care for our bodies that he does not want us swallowed up with grief, even if it is for sin (2 Corinthians 2:7). He sets boundaries on sorrow for sin – how much more then on outward sorrow for material loss? Your stores of natural strength should be used for better purposes, do you agree? The time may come that you earnestly wish you had that health and strength again to spend for God that you now so lavishly waste and prodigally throw away on your troubles to no purpose or advantage. David's dealing with sorrow revealed a high point of wisdom, and it is undoubtedly recorded for our imitation. When his child was dead, he ceased to mourn, arose, washed himself, and ate bread (2 Samuel 12:20).

5. When affliction sours the spirit with discontent and makes it inwardly resent the hand of God, then our sorrow is full of sin, and we ought to be humbled for it before the Lord. Whatever God does with us or ours, we should still maintain good thoughts of him. A gracious heart holds nearer and nearer to God in affliction, and can justify God in his severe strokes and acknowledge them all to be just and holy: *I know, O Lord, that thy judgments are right, and that thou in faithfulness hast afflicted me* (Psalm 119:75). By this, the soul may comfortably evidence to itself its own uprightness and sincere love of God. It has been of great help to some souls to take right measures of their love for God in such trials. To have lovely and pleasing thoughts of God, even when he strikes us in our nearest and dearest comforts, argues plainly that we love him for himself and not only for his gifts. His interest in the heart is deeper than any human interest is. Those who have discovered this of their own hearts during times of harsh afflictions have felt such comfort from it that they would not part with it even if they could have their friends or comforts back in place of it.

But to swell with secret discontent and have harsh thoughts of God as if he had done us wrong or dealt more severely with us than others – oh, this is a vile attitude. This cursed fruit of discontent springs from the evil root of a very carnal, ignorant, and proud heart. If the heart is renewed, it at least is very diseased and disordered. So it was with Jonah when God took his gourd: *I do well to be angry, even unto death* (Jonah 4:9). Poor man! He was highly unsettled at this time and out of sorts. This was not his true character or ordinary nature. It was a surprise, the effect of a sudden attack of temptation in which his passions had been over-excited.

Few dare to vent it in such language, but how many people have their hearts embittered by discontent and secret rebellion against the Lord? If the Lord opened their eyes to see, they would see that this discontent and rebellion will cause them more trouble than the affliction did that they are complaining about.

I do not deny that even the best heart may be tempted to think and speak disobediently concerning these works of the Lord. The envious adversary, the devil, will fan the flames and work to inflame our spirits into great discontent. The temptation was strong even on David to think harsh thoughts of God and to conclude, *Verily I have cleansed my heart in vain* (Psalm 73:13). Our godliness does little to protect us from the worst of evils. But David soon suppressed such ideas: *If I say, I will speak thus; behold, I should offend against the generation of thy children* (Psalm 73:15). By this, he meant that he would condemn the whole race of godly people through the whole world because they all have been, or perhaps will be, as severely afflicted as he was.

Surely it is meet to be said unto God, I have borne chastisement, I will not offend any more (Job 34:31). Whatever God does with you, speak well and think well of him and his actions.

6. Our sorrows exceed their proper bounds when we willingly and continually excite and renew them. Grief, like a lion, loves to play with us before it destroys us. It is strange that we should find some kind of pleasure in rousing our sorrows, but it was Seneca's observation, and experimentally true, that even sorrow itself has a certain kind of delight attending it. In relating the story of the death of Lazarus, John states that when Mary hastily ran out of the house, the Jews, who were in the house to comfort her, said, *She goeth unto the grave to weep there* (John 11:31). John Calvin says that those who go to the grave or often look on the dead body are seeking to provoke and rekindle their troubles.[2]

So, we delight to look at the reminders of our deceased friends and often talk about what they did and what they said. We do this not so much for holy and solemn instruction or imitation, for that would justify and commend the action; but instead, we do it to rub the wound and pull fresh blood from it by piercing ourselves with some trivial yet wounding facts. I have known many that will sit and talk together of the features, actions, and sayings of their children for hours, and weep at the rehearsal of them many months after they are gone. They keep the wound continually open, tormenting their own hearts, without any benefit to them. They keep a lock of hair or some other such trifle; they look on it, and it daily renews their sorrows. For this reason, Jacob would not have his son called Benoni, "the son of my sorrow." He instead called him Benjamin, so the name would not renew his sorrow (Genesis 35:18).

I am far from recommending brutish oblivion of our dear loved ones and condemn it as much as I do this childish and unprofitable remembrance. O friends, we have other things to do under the rod than these. When God's rod is on us, it is much better to be searching our hearts and houses and studying how

---

[2] John Calvin (1509–1564) was a French theologian and reformer best known for his *Institutes of the Christian Religion,* a work that became the basis of the teachings of Calvinism.

to end its strokes by ending and denying the sins and corruptions that provoke them. The rod will not be kind until this happens.

7. Lastly, our sorrows may be pronounced sinful when they deafen our ears to all the wholesome and appropriate words of counsel and comfort offered to us for our relief and support. *A voice was heard in Ramah, lamentation, and bitter weeping; Rachel weeping for her children refused to be comforted for her children, because they were not* (Jeremiah 31:15). She will allow no comfort; her disease is curable only by the restoration of her children. Give them to her again and she will be quiet. If you do not, you speak into the air; she will not listen to anything you say.

It was the same with Israel in their cruel bondage in Egypt. Moses brought them the glad news of deliverance, *but they hearkened not unto Moses for anguish of spirit, and for cruel bondage* (Exodus 6:9).

Many are so obstinately fixed in their sorrow that no words of advice or comfort find any place with them. I have known some who were exceedingly quick and ingenious, above what you would expect from them, in inventing strategies and framing objections to ward off comfort from themselves, as if they had been hired to plead against their own interest. Even if they are driven from those pleas, they are settled in their sorrow too securely to be moved. Say what you will, they are not listening. If they do hear you, your words do not stay with them. Even if it is proper, seasonable advice or comfort that is offered, they refuse it; your counsel is good, but they have no heart to hear it now. *My soul refused to be comforted* (Psalm 77:2).

To be without comfort in the time of affliction is an aggravation of our affliction, but to refuse comfort when it is offered to us is sinful. The time may come when we would be glad to receive comfort or hear a word of support, but it will be denied to us.

It is a mercy to the afflicted to have a comforter like Barnabas with them, an interpreter, one among a thousand; but those afflicted will be guilty of great sin and foolishness if, out of a disobedient and rebellious spirit, they spill on the ground like water those healing medicines of comfort that are prepared and offered to them. Do not say with them, *My strength and my hope is perished from the* LORD: *remembering mine affliction and my misery, the wormwood and the gall* (Lamentations 3:18-19). It is a thousand pities that the wormwood and gall of affliction should so disgust Christians that they would not at any time be able to relish the sweetness that is in Christ and in the promises.

I now have concluded the first part of my argument. I have shown you where the sin of mourners does and does not lie.

Chapter 3

God's Sovereignty

I have shown you where the sin and danger lie, so my way is now prepared to dissuade mourners from these sinful excesses of sorrows and to persuade them to keep the bridle of moderation on their emotions in times of affliction. I pray that my words may have as much success on those meditative souls that read them as did Abigail's on David, who, when he perceived how proper and appropriate they were, said, *Blessed be the* Lord *God of Israel, which sent thee this day to meet me: and blessed be thy advice* (1 Samuel 25:32-33).

I am aware of what a difficult task I am undertaking in trying to charm down and allay mutinous, raging, and tumultuous passions. To try to block the torrent of passion ordinarily just provokes it and makes it rage and swell even more.

The work is the Lord's; it depends entirely on his power and blessing. He who says, *Be still* to the sea when the waves roar, can also quiet and compose the stormy and tumultuous sea that rages in the hearts of the afflicted, and casts up nothing but the froth of vain and useless complaints of our misery or the dirt of sinful and wicked complaints against the actions of the Lord.

The rod of affliction goes around and visits all sorts of people with impartiality. It lands on the homes of the just and the unjust, the righteous and the wicked. Both mourn under the rod.

We should not pay so much attention to the godly that we completely neglect the ungodly. They have as strong and tender, though not as spiritual, feelings for their relatives and must not be allowed to sink completely under their unrelieved burdens.

Therefore, here I must recognize two sorts of people whom I find in tears for the same reason: both the regenerate and the unregenerate lose their dear loved ones. I am a debtor to both and will aim at their support and assistance, for even the unregenerate call for our help and pity and must not be neglected and slighted in their afflictions. We must pity those who cannot pity themselves. The law of God commands us to help a beast if it falls under its burden. How much more should we help a man who is sinking under a load of sorrows?

I confess that uses of comfort to the unregenerate are not ordinarily in use among us, and it may seem strange that anything of support can be drawn for them from Christ or the promises in which they have no special interest.

I also confess that I find myself at a great disadvantage

for this work; I cannot offer them those reviving comforts that are contained in Christ and the covenant for God's afflicted people. But the goodness of God, even to his enemies, is such that they are not left completely without support or means to soothe their sorrow.

If this is you, if you are afflicted and unsanctified, mourning bitterly for your dead friends with even more cause to mourn for your dead soul, Christless and graceless, as well as childless or friendless, if you have no comfort now or any hope in the future, if you are full of trouble and unable by prayer or faith to ease your heart – poor creature! Your situation is sad, but do not sink and allow yourself to be swallowed up with grief. You have laid your dear one in the grave, but do not throw yourself headlong into the grave after him. That will not remedy your misery, but sit down a while and ponder these three things.

First, you need to realize that of all people in the world, you have the most reason to be concerned about your life and health, and so be careful to preserve it, for if your troubles destroy you, you are eternally lost and undone forever. The apostle Paul said, *The sorrow of the world worketh death* (2 Corinthians 7:10). If it works your death, it works your damnation also, for hell follows that pale horse of death (Revelation 6:8).

> Do not put the candle of sorrow too near that thread by which you hang over the mouth of hell.

If believers die, there is no danger of hell to them. The second death has no power over them, but woe to you if it strikes you in your sin. Therefore, be very careful what you do against your health and life. Do not put the candle of sorrow too near that thread by which you hang over the mouth of hell. Oh, it is far better to be childless or friendless on earth than hopeless and without cure in hell.

Second, admit and admire the bounty and goodness of God shown to you in this affliction. When death came into your family to strike and carry off one, it was not you who was chosen to be the person. Your husband, wife, or child is taken, but you are left. If your name had been on the order, you would now be past hope!

Oh, the sparing mercy of God! The wonderful long-suffering of God toward you! Perhaps that poor creature who is gone never provoked God as you have done. Your poor child never abused mercies, neglected duties, or accumulated the ten-thousandth part of guilt that you have done, so you can easily imagine that death should have cut you down who had so provoked God instead of your poor little one.

But oh, the admirable patience of God! Oh, the riches of his long-suffering! You are only warned, not struck by it. Is there nothing in this worth being thankful for? Is it not better to be in black for someone else on earth than be in the blackness of darkness forever? Is it not easier to go to the grave of your dead friend and weep there than to go to hell among the damned where there is weeping and wailing and gnashing of teeth (Luke 13:28)?

Third, this affliction for which you mourn may be the greatest mercy ever shown to you in this world. God has now made your heart soft by trouble. He showed you the vanity of this world and what a poor trifle it was on which you based your happiness. There is now a dark cloud spread over all your worldly comforts. Oh, now if the Lord would come with this affliction, and by it open your eyes to see your deplorable state, and take your heart forever from this vain world that you now see has nothing in it, and cause you to choose Christ, the only lasting good for your happiness and inheritance; and if now your affliction will bring your sin to remembrance and your dead friend bring you to a sense of your dead soul, which is as cold to God and spiritual things as his body is to you and more loathsome in God's eyes than that corpse is or shortly will be to the eyes of men – then this day is certainly a day of the greatest mercy you have ever seen! It is a happy death that will give life to your soul!

This is sometimes how the Lord deals with people: *If they be bound in fetters, and be holden in cords of affliction; then he sheweth them their work, and their transgressions that they have exceeded. He openeth also their ear to discipline, and commandeth that they return from iniquity* (Job 36:8-10).

Oh, think and consider. The one who stole away your heart from God is now gone. The one who ate up your time and thoughts so that there was no room for God, soul, or eternity in them is gone. All the vain expectations that you raised from that poor creature which now lies in the dust are in one day gone. What an advantage you now have for heaven beyond what you had before! If God will just bless this rod, you will have cause to make this day a day of thanksgiving.

Ponder these three things. I cannot give you any other comforts because your lost condition keeps the best comforts from you. They belong to the people of God, and of yet, you have nothing to do with them.

So I will now turn from you to the people of God and present some finer comforts to them to whom they properly belong. These may be of great benefit for you to read, even if they just convince you of the blessed privilege and state of the people of God in the deepest times of trouble in this world, and what advantages of peace and contentment their share in Christ gives them that you do not have.

Here, with much more freedom and hope of success, I apply myself to the work of counseling and comforting the afflicted. You are the fearers of the Lord and tremble at his Word. The smallest sin is more alarming to you than the greatest affliction. I have no doubt you would choose to bury all your children rather than provoke and grieve your heavenly Father. Your loved ones are dear, but Christ is dearer to you by far.

Well then, let me persuade you to go for a while into your prayer closets, redeem a little time from your unprofitable sorrows, ease and empty your hearts before the Lord, and beg his blessing on the relieving, quieting, and heart-calming considerations that follow. Some of these are more general and common; some are more particular and special, but all of them, through the blessing of God, may be very useful to your souls at this time.

Consideration 1. In this day of sorrow, consider who is

the designer and author of this rod by which you now ache. Is it not the Lord? And if the Lord has done it, it is proper for you to meekly submit. *Be still, and know that I am God* (Psalm 46:10).

Humans stand on even ground. If your fellow creature does anything that displeases you, you may ask not only who did it but also why. You may demand grounds and reasons for what they have done, but you may not do so here. This one idea, *that the Lord has done it,* should, without any further disputes or contests, silence and quiet you no matter what it is that he has done. *Why dost thou strive against him? for he giveth not account of any of his matters* (Job 33:13). The Supreme Being must be a Being that cannot be held to account or controlled.

It is a shame for children to struggle with their fathers and a shame for servants to contend with their masters, but for a creature to quarrel and strive with the God who made him – how shameful it is! Certainly, it is highly reasonable that you would be subject to that will from which you originated, and that he who formed you and yours should do with both as he sees fit. The author of the book of Samuel said, *Whatsoever the king did pleased all the people* (2 Samuel 3:36). Should anything the Lord does displease you? He can do no wrong.

If we pluck a rose in the bud as we walk in our gardens, who will criticize us for it? It belongs to us, and we can cut it off when we please. It is the same in your situation. Your sweet bud, which was cut off before it was fully grown, was cut off by him who owned it, by him who created and formed it.

If his dominion is absolute, then certainly what he does should be acceptable. It was so to good Eli: *It is the LORD: let him do what seemeth him good* (1 Samuel 3:18). It was so to David: *I was dumb, I opened not my mouth; because thou didst it* (Psalm 39:9). Let it be forever remembered that he, *whose name alone is JEHOVAH, art the most high over all the earth* (Psalm 83:18).

God illustriously displays his glorious sovereignty in two things: his decrees and his providences. Concerning his decrees, he says, *I will have mercy on whom I will have mercy* (Romans 9:15). There are no grounds to dispute with him. Paul asks, *O man, who art thou that repliest against God? Shall the thing formed say to him that formed it, Why hast thou made me thus? Hath not the potter power over the clay?* (Romans 9:20-21).

> We have acknowledged that the Lord has brought the affliction, if it had not been his will, it could never have been done.

As to his providence, which also displays his sovereignty, it is written in Zechariah, *Be silent, O all flesh, before the LORD: for he is raised up out of his holy habitation* (Zechariah 2:13). Scripture speaks of his providential work in the changes of kingdoms and the devastation that accompanies them.

Now, so far, we have acknowledged that the Lord has brought the affliction, it is his pleasure to have it as it is, and if it had not been his will, it could never have been done. He who gave you (actually, lent you) your loved ones, has also taken them. This consideration should leave you so quiet! If your landlord, who for many years has allowed you to live in his house, now gives you notice that you must leave, even though he gives you no reason, you will not contend with him or say he has done you wrong. You would be even less likely to contend with him if he were to tell you that it will be better and more profitable for him to take it into his own hand than to rent it to you any longer. Undoubtedly, reason will tell you that you ought to quietly pack up and leave.

It is your great landlord, at whose pleasure you hold your own and your relatives' lives, who has now given you notice from one of them, perhaps because it may be more for his glory to take the person in death. And you think you must dispute the case with him?

Come, Christian, this in no way is consistent with who you are. *The LORD gave, and the LORD hath taken away; blessed be the name of the LORD* (Job 1:21). Stop looking at a dead creature and lift up your eyes to the sovereign, wise, and holy will that ordered this affliction. Consider who he is and what you are. Pursue this consideration until you can say, "I am now filled with the will of God."

Consideration 2. Think carefully about the quality of the comfort you are deprived of and remember that when you had it, it ranked as a common and ordinary comfort.

Children, and all other relatives, are but common

blessings that God gives indiscriminately to his friends and enemies. You cannot tell whom God loves and hates by who has had or who has lost children. The Psalms say of the wicked, *They are full of children,* children that survive them, for they *leave the rest of their substance to their babes* (Psalm 17:14). They are full of sin, yet full of children, and these children live to inherit their parents' sins and estates together.

It is mistaking the quality and nature of our joys that so plunges us into trouble when we lose them. We think there is such a necessary connection between these creatures and our happiness that we are utterly undone when they fail us.

But this is our mistake. There is no such necessary connection or dependence. We may be happy without these things. It is not father, mother, wife, or child in which our highest good and joy lie. We have higher, better, and more enduring things than these. These may all perish, but our souls are secure and safe, and our comfort now, as well as in the end, is safe, even though these are gone.

God has better things to comfort his people with than these, and worse rods to afflict you with than the removal of these. If God had let your children live and flourish and had given you ease and rest in your home, but in the meantime inflicted spiritual judgment on your souls, how much sadder would your situation be!

As long as our best mercies are safe, the things that have salvation in them remain, and only the things that have emptiness in them are removed. You are not prejudiced or much hindered in the attainment of your eternal future by the loss of these things.

It was not Christ's intent to purchase physical contentment for you with these earthly comforts, but to redeem you from all iniquity, purge your sins, sanctify your natures, wean your hearts from this vain world, and so incline and order your present condition that, finding no rest and contentment here, you might even more ardently pant and sigh after the rest which remains for the people of God. Do you think it is not as probable for you to gain this end as it was before? Do you think you are not as likely to be weaned from the world by these methods of Providence as by more pleasant and prosperous ones? Every wise man reckons that station and condition to be best for him that most advances and secures the great design and his last end.

Well then, consider that you are as well without these things as with them. You are even better if they were obstructions and snares to your affections. You have not really lost anything if the things in which your eternal happiness consists are still safe. Many of God's dearest children have been denied comforts such as these, and many have been deprived of them, yet they were never farther from Christ and heaven because of that.

Consideration 3. Always remember that no matter how soon and unexpected the parting with your loved ones was, your lease was expired before you lost them, and you enjoyed them every moment of the time that God intended for you to have them.

Even before this loved one whose loss you lament was born, the time of your joy and separation was unalterably fixed and appointed in heaven by the God of the spirits of all flesh. Although it was a secret to you while your loved one was with you, it now is a plain and evident thing that this was the appointed time of separation and that the life of your loved one could by no means be prolonged or shortened, but must keep you company just so long and then part from you.

This position has full and clear scriptural authority for its foundation. How significant and full is that text in Job: *Seeing his days are determined, the number of his months are with thee, thou hast appointed his bounds that he cannot pass* (Job 14:5).

The length of our life, as well as the place of our residence, was fixed before we were born. To be well established in this truth will contribute greatly to your contentment and peace. The appointed time was fully come when you and your loved one parted. Knowing this will prevent and save a great deal of trouble that comes from our reflections. "Oh, if I had done this or not done that, then my dear husband, wife, or child would still be alive today!" No, the Lord's time was fully come, and all things agreed and fell in together to bring about the pleasure of his will. Let that satisfy you. Even if the finest physicians in the world had been there, or had those who were there prescribed another course, the outcome would have been the same. I must caution you though, that the decree of God in no way excuses any voluntary or sinful neglects or failures. God overrules these things to serve his own ends, but he does not approve of them. But it greatly comforts us to know that even if we had corrected all our involuntary and unavoidable oversights and mistakes about the means of care or the timing of them, things would still be as they are now.

There are objections to this position that seem to have support from Scriptures such as these: *Bloody and deceitful men shall not live out half their days* (Psalm 55:23); *Why shouldest thou die before thy time?* (Ecclesiastes 7:17); *O my God, take me not away in the midst of my days* (Psalm 102:24); *I am deprived of the residue of my years* (Isaiah 38:10); *The fear of the LORD prolongeth days: but the years of the wicked shall be shortened* (Proverbs 10:27). What satisfactory sense can we give to these Scriptures while we also assert an unalterable fixing of the time of death?

The satisfying solution will be found by distinguishing between death and its terms. First, we must distinguish natural death from violent death. Wicked and bloodthirsty men will not live out half their days, that is, half as long as they might live according to the course of nature or the vigor and soundness of their natural constitution. Their wickedness either drowns nature in an excess of extravagance and luxury, or exposes them to the hand of justice that will execute punishment for their wickedness before they have lived half their days.

Second, we need to distinguish the general terms

or limit for death from the special. The general limits are now seventy or eighty years: *The days of our years are threescore years and ten; and if by reason of strength they be fourscore years, yet is their strength labour and sorrow* (Psalm 90:10). Since the flood, the life of humans is generally held to this short limit, and though there are a few exceptions, the general rule stands.

The special limit is that measure of time that God, by his own counsel and will, has allotted to every individual person. It is known to us only when death occurs. We affirm this to be a fixed and immovable term. With it, all things will fall into place and we will observe the will of God in our death at that time.

Because the general limit is known and the special limit is a secret hidden with God, man counts by the former limit and may be said, when they die at thirty or forty years old, to be cut off in the midst of their days. They are cut off in the middle if we are counting by the general account, though they are not cut off until the end of their days if we determine by the special limit. So the wicked die before their time, the time that they might attain in an ordinary life, but they do not die before the time God has appointed. It is the same in all the other objected Scriptures.

It is not proper at all in a subject of this nature to digress into a controversy. The poor mourners, overwhelmed with grief, have no pleasure in that. It is not proper for them at this time, so for the present, I will waive the controversy and close this consideration with a humble and serious recommendation to the afflicted to wisely consider the matter. The Lord's time had come.

God set their time before you even had them, and your loved ones lived with you every moment of that time.

O parents! I beg you to pay attention to this. The length of your child's time in the womb was fixed to a minute by the Lord, and when the ordained fullness of that time was come, were you not willing that your child would be delivered into the world? The tender mother would not have it stay one minute longer in the womb no matter how much she loved it. For the same reason, we should be willing, when God's appointed time has come, to have it delivered by death out of this state which, in respect of the life of heaven, is but as the life of a child in the womb to its life in the open world.

Do not let anyone say the death of a child is a premature death. God has ways we do not understand to ready those for heaven whom he intends to gather there before the expected time. In respect of fitness for heaven, they die at a full age even though they are cut off in the bud of their time.

He who appointed the seasons of the year also appointed the seasons of our comfort in our loved ones. These cannot be altered any more than the seasons of the year can be. The course of Providence is guided by an unalterable decree. What happens casually to our understanding, happens necessarily in respect of God's appointment. So be quieted and calmed in it. This must be just as it is.

Consideration 4. Has God struck your darling and

taken away the delight of your eyes with this stroke? Bear this stroke with patience and quiet submission, for how do you know if your sorrow might have been greater from the life of your child than it is now from the death of your child?

Sad experience made a man once say, "It is better to weep for ten dead children than for one living child. A living child may prove a continual collapse, yes, a continual dying to the parent's heart." What sad words David said to Abishai: *Behold, my son, which came forth of my bowels, seeketh my life* (2 Samuel 16:11).

I remember Seneca, in his consolatory letter to his friend Marullus, attempts to talk him out of his excessive grief. Marullus wonders, "Oh, if my child had lived with me, to what great modesty, gravity, and prudence might my discipline have formed and molded him?" Seneca answers, "Your son might have turned out temperate and prudent, but (which is more to be feared) he might have been as most others are. Look what children come out of even the worthiest families; they cater to both their own and others in mutual lusts. In all their lives, a day never passes without the mark of some shame or wickedness on it."

I know that your tender love for your children will not allow such doubts of them. They are, for the present, sweet, lovely, innocent companions, and you are sure that by your care of their education and prayer for them they might have been the joy of your heart.

Undoubtedly, Esau, when he was little and in his tender age, promised as much comfort to his parents as Jacob did. I do not question that Isaac and Rebekah, a noble pair, spent as many prayers on him and gave him as much holy teaching as they did his brother, but when the child grew up to riper years, he became a sharp affliction to his parents. It is said, *Esau was forty years old when he took to wife Judith the daughter of Beeri the Hittite, and Bashemath the daughter of Elon the Hittite: which were a grief of mind unto Isaac and to Rebekah* (Genesis 26:34-35). Those words *grief of mind* come from a root that signifies "to embitter." This child embittered the minds of his parents by his rebellion against them and by despising their counsels.

I do not doubt that Abraham disciplined his family as strictly as any of you. There was never a man that received higher praise from God on that account: *I know him, that he will command his children and his household after him, and they shall keep the way of the* LORD (Genesis 18:19). And I can only imagine that he offered as many and as frequent prayers for his children, particularly for his son Ishmael, as any of you. We find one, a very pitiful one, recorded in Genesis: *O that Ishmael might live before thee!* (Genesis 17:18), yet you know that he proved to be a son that yielded him no more comfort than Esau did to Isaac and Rebekah.

It is so much more common for parents to see the vices and evils of their children than their virtues and graces! Where one parent lives to rejoice in seeing the grace of God shining forth in the life of his child, there are twenty, it may be one hundred, who live to see, to their worry and grief, the workings of sin in them.

Plutarch, in his book *The Morals,* notes that many men do not live to see their children doing great and noble things, but men commonly live to see their children fall into gambling, reveling, drinking, and whoring. Multitudes live to see such things to their sorrow. And if you are a gracious soul, what a wound this is to your very heart! To see those, as David spoke of his Absalom, who came from your own flesh, to be sinning against God, that God whom you love and whose honor is dearer to you than your very life!

But even if they should prove to be civil and hopeful children, might you not live to see more misery come to them than you could endure seeing? Think what a sad and sorrowful sight it was to Zedekiah that the king of Babylon killed his sons before his eyes (Jeremiah 52:10). It was a horrid spectacle that leads us to the next consideration.

Consideration 5. Perhaps by this stroke which you are so lamenting, God has taken your loved one away from the evil to come.

It is God's usual way when some extraordinary calamities are coming on the world to hide some of his weak and tender ones out of the way by death (Isaiah 57:1-2). He leaves some and removes others, but he takes care of the security of all. He provided a grave for Methuselah before the flood. The grave is a hiding place to some, and God sees it better for them to be underground than above ground in such evil days.

A careful and tender father who has a son abroad at school and hears the plague has broken out in the town or near there will directly send his horse to bring home his son before the danger and difficulty become greater. In the same way, death is our Father's pale horse which he sends to bring home his tender children and carry them out of harm's way.

Certainly, when national calamities are approaching, it is far better for our friends to be in the grave in peace than exposed to the miseries and distresses which are here. This is the meaning of Jeremiah 22:10: *Weep ye not for the dead, neither bemoan him: but weep sore for him that goeth away: for he shall return no more, nor see his native country.*

Is there not a dreadful sound of trouble now in our ears? The clouds are gathering blackness. All things around us seem to be preparing and arranging themselves for affliction. The days may be near in which you will say, *Blessed are the barren, and the wombs that never bare, and the paps which never gave suck* (Luke 23:29).

It was in the day when the faith and patience of the saints were tested that John heard a voice from heaven saying to him, *Write, Blessed are the dead which die in the Lord from henceforth* (Revelation 14:13).

Your friend, by an act of favor, is removed by death, while you yourself are left to endure a great fight of affliction. Now, if troubles come, your cares and fears will be so much less, and your own death so much easier when so much of you has passed from this life to the next already. In this case, the Lord, by merciful providence, is providing both for their safety and your own easier passage to them.

In removing your friends beforehand, he seems to say to you as he did to Peter, *What I do thou knowest not now; but thou shalt know hereafter* (John 13:7). The eye of Providence has a view far beyond yours. It would probably be a harder task for you to leave them behind than to follow them. A tree that is deeply rooted in the earth requires many strokes to fell it, but when its roots are loosened beforehand, then an easy stroke lays it down on the earth.

Consideration 6. A parting time must come; this is as good a time as another. You knew beforehand that your child or friend was mortal, and that the thread that linked you together must be cut.

Basil writes that when you first became a parent, you knew, being mortal yourself, that your child was a mortal, vanishing thing. Why, then, are you astonished to see a dying thing dead? Seneca writes that he who complains that one is dead, complains that he was a man. All people are under the same condition: Those who are born must die.

We are indeed distinguished by the distance between our deaths but equalized in the issue. *It is appointed unto men once to die* (Hebrews 9:27). It is a law of heaven.

Possibly you think this is the worst time for parting that there could be. If you had enjoyed your loved one longer, you could have parted easier. But how deceived you are in that! The longer you had enjoyed them, the more unwilling you would have been to leave them, and the deeper they would have rooted themselves in your affections.

If God had given you the privilege of having the union between you and your friend not be dissolved until you were willing for it to be dissolved, when do you think you would have been willing for that to happen?

It is good for us and ours that our times are in God's hand (Psalm 31:15) and not in our own. However immature and young your loved ones seemed to be when they were cut down, they came to the *grave in a full age, like as a shock of corn cometh in in his season* (Job 5:26). Those who are in Christ and in the covenant never die unseasonably, no matter when they die.

They die in a good old age. Yes, even though they die in the spring and flower of youth, they die in a good old age. They are ripe and mature for death whenever they die. Whenever the godly die, it is harvest time for them. In their natural capacity, they are cut down while they are green and cropped in the bud or blossom. Yet in their spiritual capacity, they never die before they are ripe. God can ripen them quickly; he can let out warm rays and beams of his Holy Spirit on them that rapidly mature the seeds of grace into preparedness for glory.

It was, without a doubt, the most fit and seasonable time for your children to die, and as it is a fit time for them, so it is for you also. Had they lived longer, they might have engaged you more, so that your parting would have been harder, or else they may have confused and hobbled you more by revealing their natural corruption. What a stinging aggravation of your sorrow, then, that would have been!

Certainly, the Lord of time is the best judge of time. There is nothing we can do more to discover our folly and rashness than to presume to set the times either of our comforts or our troubles. As for our comforts, we never think they can come soon enough; we want them now, whether it is the right season or not: *Heal her now, O God* (Numbers 12:13). Let it be done quickly. We want our comforts immediately, but as for our afflictions, we never think they come late enough. Not at this time, Lord, any other time but now.

It is good to leave the timing both of the one and the other to him whose works are all beautiful in their seasons and who never does anything in an improper time.

Consideration 7. Call to mind, in this day of trouble, the covenant you have with God and what you solemnly promised him in the day you took him for your God.

It will be very timely and useful for you, Christian, at this time, to reflect on these transactions and the frame of your heart in those days when a heavier load of sorrow pressed on your heart than you feel now.

In your spiritual distress, when the burden of sin lay heavy, when the curse of the law, the fear of hell, and the dread of death and eternity attacked you on every side and kept you from Christ, the only door of hope – then you would have counted it good news to escape that danger with the loss of all your earthly comforts! Was this not your cry in those days: "Lord, give me Christ and deny me whatever else you please! Pardon my sin, save my soul, and to do both, unite me to Christ, and I will never mourn or open my mouth. Do what you will with me; let me be friendless, let me be childless, let me be poor, let me be anything, rather than a Christless, graceless, hopeless soul." When the Lord listened to your cry and showed you mercy, when he pulled you off from the world into your prayer closet and there dealt with you in secret, when he was working up your heart to the terms of his covenant and made you willing to accept Christ on his own terms – oh, then you so eagerly submitted to his yoke and considered it most reasonable and easy!

Recall those days and the secret places where Christ and you made the bargain. Were not these words, or words like them, whispered by you into his ear, with a down-turned eye and melting heart:

"Lord Jesus, here am I, a poor guilty sinner, deeply burdened with sin. Fear and trouble are on one hand, and there is a just God, a severe law, and everlasting burning on the other hand. But blessed be God! O blessed be God for Jesus the Mediator, who puts himself between me and it! You are the only door of hope through which I can escape, and your blood is the only means of my pardon and salvation. You have said, *Come unto me, all ye that labour and are heavy laden.* You have promised that he who comes to you will never be cast out (Matthew 11:28; John 6:37).

"Blessed Jesus, your poor creature comes to you based on these encouragements. I come, but it is with much stumbling. I have many doubts and fears of the outcome, yet I am willing to come and make a covenant with you this day.

"I take you this day to be my Lord and submit heartily to all that you do. Do what you will with me or mine, let me be rich or poor, let me be anything or nothing in this world; I am willing to be as you would have me, and I give myself to you this day to be yours. All I am, all I have, will be yours. It will be yours to serve you and yours to be disposed of at your pleasure. You will from now on be my highest Lord, my chief good, my last end."

Now, Christian, make good the promise to Christ that you so solemnly made. It is he who has disposed of your dear relative as it pleased him, and he is thereby testing your honesty in the covenant that you made with him. Where is the satisfaction and contentment you promised to take in all his actions? Where is that covenanted submission to his will? Did you want an exception for this affliction that has come upon you?

> If you were sincere in your covenant, you had no reserve on your part, as Christ had none on his.

Did you tell him, "Lord, I will be content in you when you take anything I have, except this husband, this wife, or this dear child; I reserve this out of the bargain. I would never endure if you were to kill this comfort." If so, you proved yourself a hypocrite. If you were sincere in your covenant, you had no reserve on your part, as Christ had none on his.

It was without any exception that you then resigned to him. Will you go back on your word as one that made too many promises and then regrets the bargain, or, at least, as one that has forgotten these solemn transactions in the days of your distress? Has Christ failed in one iota that he promised you? Charge him, if you can, with the smallest unfaithfulness. He has been completely faithful on his part; make sure you are so on yours. Today it is put to the test. Remember what you have promised him.

Consideration 8. But if your covenant with God will not quiet you, I think God's covenant with you might venture to do it.

Is your family, which was recently hopeful, flourishing, and a peaceful shelter, now broken up and scattered? Are your offspring, whom you expected to provide you great comfort in your old age, cut off, so that you are now likely neither to have a name nor a memorial left to you in the earth? Do you sit alone and mourn to think what has become of your hopes and comforts now? Do you read over these words of Job and comment on them with many tears: *Oh that I were as in months past, as in the days when God preserved me; when his candle shined upon my head, and when by his light I walked through darkness; as I was in the days of my youth, when the secret of God was upon my tabernacle; when the Almighty was yet with me, when my children were about me* (Job 29:2-5)?

Let the covenant God has made with you comfort you in your desolate condition. You know what domestic troubles David met with in a sad succession, not only from the death of children, but, what was much worse, also from the wicked lives of his children. There was incest, murder, and rebellion in his family, a far more painful trial than death in their infancy could have been, but see how sweetly he gains relief from the covenant of grace: *Although my house be not so with God; yet he hath made with me an everlasting covenant, ordered in all things, and sure: for this is all my salvation, and all my desire, although he make it not to grow* (2 Samuel 23:5).

I know that this text principally refers to Christ who was to spring out of David's family according to God's covenant made with him on that behalf, but I think that it has another, though less principal, respect to his own family and the afflictions and troubles over which the covenant of God with him did abundantly comfort him. Although his house did not increase, and those that were left were not as he desired, David was comforted by the covenant. Whatever troubles or deaths are in your families, those of you who have a share in the covenant can be abundantly comforted by it also. We can be sure of this for three reasons.

> You are as much on his heart in your deepest afflictions as in the greatest flourish of your prosperity.

First, if you are God's covenant people, he may afflict you, but he will never forget you. *He will ever be mindful of his covenant* (Psalm 111:5). You are as much on his heart in your deepest afflictions as in the greatest flourish of your prosperity.

You find it hard to forget your children, even though they now are turned to a heap of corruption and loathsome rottenness. Oh, how your mind runs on them night and day! Your thoughts never grow tired of that subject. But certainly, it is easier for you to forget your dear child while living and most endearing (much more when dead and undesirable) than it is for your God to forget you. *Can a woman forget her sucking child, that she should not have compassion on the son of her womb? yea, they may forget, yet will I not forget thee* (Isaiah 49:15).

Can a woman forget her nursing child, her own child? Her own child, while it hangs on her breast, together with the milk from her breast, draws love from its mother's heart. Is it possible for her to forget? It may be possible because human love is fickle and variable. But *will I not forget thee;* it is an everlasting covenant.

Second, as he will never forget you in your troubles, so he will order all your troubles for your good. It is a well-ordered covenant, or a covenant divinely disposed so that everything will work together for your good (Romans 8:28).

The covenant directs all your trials and your various troubles so that they will sweetly cooperate and join their united influences to make you happy.

Possibly you cannot see how your present affliction can be for your good. You are ready to say with Jacob, *Joseph is not, and Simeon is not, and ye will take Benjamin away: all these things are against me* (Genesis 42:36);

but if you could just once see how sweetly and orderly all these afflictions work under the blessing and influence of the covenant to your eternal good, you would not only be quiet, but you would also be thankful for those things that now so much afflict and trouble you.

Third, this covenant is not only well ordered in all things, but it is also sure. The mercies contained in it are called *the sure mercies of David* (Isaiah 55:3). This consideration gives such a sweet and appropriate support to God's afflicted people under the rod! Recently, you made yourselves sure of that human comfort who has forsaken you. It may be that you said of your child who is now gone, as Lamech said of his son Noah, *This same shall comfort us concerning our work and toil of our hands* (Genesis 5:29). He meant that their son would not only comfort them by assisting them in the work of their hands, but also in enjoying the fruit of their toil and pains for him.

You have probably had such thoughts and raised great expectations of comfort in your old age from it, but now you see that you built on the sand. Where would you be now if you had not a firmer base to build on? But, blessed be God, the covenant mercies are more sure and solid! God, Christ, and heaven never waver as these things do.

The sweetest human joys you ever had or have in this world cannot say to you as your God does, *I will never leave thee, nor forsake thee* (Hebrews 13:5). You must part with your dear husband, however much you love him. You must say goodbye to the wife you love, no matter how well your emotions are linked and how much your heart delights in her. Your children and you must be separated even though they are to you as your own soul.

Though these vanish away, blessed be God, there is something that stays. Though all flesh is as grass and the beauty of it as the flower of the grass, though the grass withers and its flower fades because the Spirit of the Lord blows on it, yet the word of our God will stand forever (Isaiah 40:6-8). There is so much support contained in this one thought, that if you could just fix your faith here, to realize and apply it, I might lay down my pen at this point and say the work is done. Nothing more is needed.

Consideration 9. The hope of the resurrection should powerfully restrain all excesses of sorrow in those that do profess that hope.

Only those who mourn without hope should mourn without end. The gardener does not mourn when he casts his seed corn into the earth because he sows in hope. He commits it to the ground with an expectation to receive it again with improvement. That is the case here. The apostle Paul states, *But I would not have you to be ignorant, brethren, concerning them which are asleep, that ye sorrow not, even as others which have no hope. For if we believe that Jesus died and rose again, even so them also which sleep in Jesus will God bring with him* (1 Thessalonians 4:13-14).

> Do not look on the dead as a lost generation.

Do not look on the dead as a lost generation. Do not

think that death has annihilated and utterly destroyed them. They are not dead, they are only asleep. And if they sleep, they will awake again. You do not wail and cry out for your children and friends when you find them asleep on their beds. Why, death is just a longer sleep out of which they will awake as certainly as they did in the morning in this world.

I have often wondered at that golden sentence in Seneca: "My thoughts of the dead are not as others are. I have fair and pleasant appreciations of them, for I enjoyed them as one that knew he must part with them, and I part with them as one that expects to have them."

No doubt he speaks of the enjoyment of them that he would have from his pleasant contemplations of their virtuous actions, for he was entirely unacquainted with the comfortable and heart-strengthening doctrine of the resurrection. If he had known the advantages that result from knowing the resurrection, can you imagine how enthusiastically he would have spoken of the dead and of their state? You profess to believe this, but you enthusiastically sorrow! Oh, do not allow paganism to outdo Christianity. Do not let pagans challenge the greatest believers and surpass them in quiet and cheerful behavior under affliction.

I beg you, if your deceased friend has left you any solid ground of hope that he died sharing in Christ and the covenant, to distinctly ponder these admirable supports that the doctrine of the resurrection affords:

1. The same body that was so pleasant a sight to you will be restored again. Yes, specifically the same, so that it will not only be what it was, but also who it was. *Mine eyes shall behold, and not another* (Job 19:27). The very same body you laid, or are now about to lay, in the grave, will be restored again. You will find your own husband, wife, child, or friend again. I say, exactly the same and not another.

2. Further, as you will see the same people who were so dear to you, so you will know them to be the same who were once so dear to you on earth and so closely related. You will not know them any longer in a physical relationship; death has dissolved that bond. But you will know them to be those who were once your dear relatives in this world and be able to single them out among that great multitude and say, "This was my father, mother, husband, wife, and child. These were the people for whom I wept and prayed, who were instruments of good to me or to whose salvation God made me instrumental."

For in heaven, we will have all the cumulative knowledge and whatever knowledge that will certainly perfect, enlarge, and heighten our happiness and satisfaction. Martin Luther, asked about this point at supper the evening before he died, replied, "What happened to Adam? He never saw Eve; he was in a deep sleep when God formed her. But when he awoke and saw her, he did not ask what she was or from where she came. Instead, he said she was flesh of his flesh and bone of his bone. How did he know that? He was full of the Holy Spirit and endowed with the knowledge of God." In the same manner, we will in the other life be renewed by Christ and will know our parents, our wives, and our children.

And this, among other things, was how Augustine comforted Lady Italica after the death of her husband. He told her that she would know him in the world to come among the glorified saints. Someone greater than either Luther or Augustine – the apostle Paul – comforted himself by saying that the Thessalonians, whom he had converted to Christ, would be his hope, joy, and crown of rejoicing *in the presence of our Lord Jesus Christ at his coming* (1 Thessalonians 2:19), which implies his distinct knowledge of them in that day that must be many hundred years after death has separated them from each other.

We do not know if this knowledge will be by glorified eyes discerning facial features or some individuality remaining on the glorified bodies of our relatives, or if it will be by immediate revelation as Adam knew his wife and as Peter, James, and John knew Moses and Elijah on the mount. As it is difficult to determine, it is pointless to puzzle ourselves about it.

That we will have such a knowledge of them in heaven is the existing judgment of sound theologians, and it has support from Scripture and reason. The sadness of this parting will be abundantly compensated by the joy of that meeting. This is especially true considering the next point.

3. At our next meeting, they will be unspeakably more

desirable, sweet, and excellent than they ever were in this world. They had a desirableness in them here, but they were not altogether lovely or in every respect desirable. They had their infirmities, both natural and moral, but all these are removed in heaven and forever done away. No natural infirmities hang around glorified bodies or sinful ones on perfected spirits of the just. What lovely creatures they will appear to you then when that which is now sown in dishonor will be raised in honor (1 Corinthians 15:43).

4. To crown all, you will have an everlasting enjoyment of them in heaven, never to part again. The children of the resurrection can die no more (Luke 20:36). You will kiss their pale lips and cold cheeks no more. You will never fear another parting pull, but will be together with the Lord forever (1 Thessalonians 4:17). The apostle thought this was a healing comfort when he exhorted the Thessalonians to *comfort one another with these words* (1 Thessalonians 4:18).

Consideration 10. The present happiness into which all that die in Christ are presently admitted should abundantly comfort Christians over the death of those that either carried a lively hope out of the world with them or have left good grounds of such a hope behind them.

There are some that carried a lively hope to heaven with them and who could evidence to themselves and friends their saving interest in Christ and in the covenant. Even though they died in silence, their conversations and conduct would have spoken for them, and the character of their lives leaves no grounds of doubt concerning their death. Others, dying in their infancy and youth, though they did not carry such an actual hope with them, have left good grounds of hope behind them.

Parents, please ponder these grounds. You have prayed for them; you have many times wrestled with the Lord on their behalf. You have taken hold of God's covenant for them, as well as for yourselves, and dedicated them to the Lord. They have not, by any actions of theirs, destroyed those grounds of your hope. You may, with much probability, conclude that they are with God. If that be the case, what abundant reasons you have to be quiet and satisfied with what God has done. Can they be better than where they are? Did you have better provisions and entertainment for them here than their heavenly Father has above?

There are no Christian parents in the world who would not rejoice to see their children outrun and get ahead of them in grace so that their children may be more notable in abilities and service than they ever were. What reason can be given why we should not as much rejoice to see our children get ahead of us in glory as in grace? Their life on earth was finished a few years before you. Is that a matter of mourning? Would not your child say, as Christ did to his friends a little before his death when he saw them discouraged at the thought of parting, *If ye loved me, ye would rejoice, because I said, I go unto the Father* (John 14:28)? He says, "Do not value your own physical comfort from my bodily presence with you more than my glory and advancement in heaven. Is this love for me? Or is it instead self-love?"

Your departed child might say to you, "You have said all along that you love me very much; my happiness seemed to be very dear to you. Why, then, do you mourn so excessively now? This is the effect of a foolish and physical love rather than of a rational and spiritual love. If you loved me with a pure spiritual love, you would rejoice that I have gone to my Father. It is infinitely better for me to be here, than with you on earth under sin and sorrow. Do not weep for me, but weep for yourselves."

Even though you want your children's company, they do not want yours. Your care was to provide for your children, but Jesus Christ has provided infinitely better for them than you could. You intended an estate, but Christ provided a kingdom. You thought on such and such a match, but Christ has forbidden all others and married your child to himself. Can you imagine a higher promotion for the fruit of your bodies?

A king from heaven has sent for your child; do you resent that he has gone? Think again of what an honor it is to you that Christ has taken him out of your care and protection and laid him in his own. He stripped him out of those garments you provided and clothed him in white robes washed in the blood of the Lamb. Do not let your hearts be troubled. Instead, rejoice exceedingly that God made you instruments to replenish heaven and bring forth an heir for the kingdom of God.

Your child is now glorifying God in a higher way than you can, and though you have lost his bodily presence for a time, I hope you do not count something that turns to God's greater glory to be your loss.

When Jacob heard his Joseph was lord of Egypt, he wished himself to be with Joseph rather than his Joseph to be with him in need and dire straits. It should be the same way with you. You are still rolling and tossing on a tempestuous sea, but your loved ones have gone into the quiet harbor. Desire to be where they are and not that they were here at sea again with you.

Consideration 11. Consider how vain all your troubles and worry are. They in no way better your situation or ease your burden.

By wrestling and sweating in the field, a bull makes his yoke heavier, chafes his neck, spends his strength sooner, and in no way helps himself. Why are you doing the same thing? If you are like a bull unaccustomed to the yoke (Jeremiah 31:18), what Christ says of caring, we may say of grieving: *Which of you by taking thought can add one cubit unto his stature?* (Matthew 6:27).

Cares may interrupt our sleep and break our hearts, but they cannot add to our stature either physically or in the eyes of people. Our sorrow may sooner break our hearts than the yoke God has laid on you.

All this is as the fluttering of a bird caught in a net. Instead of freeing itself, this entangles the bird even more. When God signified his will in the death of David's child, David wisely resolved: *But now he is dead, wherefore should I fast? can I bring him back again? I shall go to him, but he shall not return to me* (2 Samuel 12:23).

Can I bring him back again? No, I can no more alter the purpose and work of God than I can change the seasons of the year, alter the course of the sun, moon, and stars, or disturb the order of day and night. All are unalterably established by a firm constitution and decree of heaven.

These seasons cannot be changed by man, neither will God change the course and way of his providence. *He is in one mind, and who can turn him? and what his soul desireth, even that he doeth* (Job 23:13). While his pleasure and purpose are unknown to us, there is room for fasting and prayer to prevent the thing we fear. But when the purpose of God is demonstrated in the outcome and the stroke is given, then it is the vainest thing in the world to fret and distress ourselves. David's servants thought that is what he would do as soon as he heard that the child was dead. But he was wiser than that. His tears and cries to God before the child died had the nature and proper means to try to prevent the affliction, but when the affliction came and could not be prevented, then they were of no use, no purpose in the world. *Wherefore should I fast?* To what end, use, or purpose will it be now?

Do not throw away your strength and spirits for no reason. Reserve them for future tests and trials. The time may come that you will need all the strength you have, and much more, to support a greater burden than this.

Consideration 12. If you meekly submit to him and patiently wait for him under the rod, the Lord is able to doubly restore all your lost comforts in friends and family.

When Esau lost his blessing, he said, *Hast thou but one blessing, my father?* (Genesis 27:38). But your Father has more than one blessing for you; his name is *the Father of mercies* (2 Corinthians 1:3). He can create and bring about as many mercies for you as he pleases. Loved ones and their comforts are at his command.

Just a few months or years ago, these joys, whose loss you now mourn, were not even in existence, nor did you know they would come to you, but the Lord gave the word and commanded them for you. And, if he pleases, he can make the death of these like a scythe to the meadow that is mown down or a razor to the head that is shaved bare. Though it lay you under the present trouble and reproach of barrenness, it makes a way for a double increase, a second spring with profit.

So it was with the captive church in respect to her special children in the day of her captivity and reproach. The Lord made up all her loss and more, even to her own astonishment. *The children which thou shalt have, after thou hast lost the other, shall say again in thine ears, The place is too strait for me: give place to me that I may dwell* (Isaiah 49:20). He may deal the same way with you concerning your natural children and relatives so that what the man of God said to Amaziah may be applied to you: *Amaziah said to the man of God, But what shall we do for the hundred talents which I have given to the army of Israel? And the man of God answered, The Lord is able to give thee much more than this* (2 Chronicles 25:9).

Do not ask, "What will I do for friends and relatives? Death has robbed me of all comfort from them." The Lord is able to give you much more. But as you expect to see your future blessings multiplied, be careful that you neither dishonor God nor grieve him by your disobedient and impatient conduct under the present rod.

God took away all Job's children in one immediate and extraordinary stroke. They were, at least some of them, grown and planted in distinct families and they were struck while they were caring for and loving each other. This was an extraordinary trial, yet Job meekly receives and patiently bears it from the hand of the Lord.

Ye have heard of the patience of Job, and have seen the end of the Lord (James 5:11). We see not only the gracious end or intention of the Lord in all his afflictions, but also the happy end and outcome the Lord gave to all his afflictions. The account in Job says, *The Lord gave Job twice as much as he had before* (Job 42:10). The number of his children was not doubled as all his other comforts were, but though the Lord only restored the same number to him that he took away, it is likely the comforts he had in these latter children were double what he had in the former. There is nothing lost by waiting patiently and submitting willingly to the Lord's determinations.

The Lord can just as easily revive as remove your comforts in your loved ones. There is a sweet expression to this purpose in Psalm 18:28: *For thou wilt light my candle: the Lord my God will enlighten my darkness.* Every comfortable joy, whether it be in relatives, estate, health, or friends, is a candle lighted by Providence for our comfort in this world. They are just candles. They will not always last, and those that last longest will eventually be consumed and used up. But often with them, as with candles, they are blown out before they are half-consumed, almost as soon as they were lit, and then we are in darkness for the present.

It is a dark hour for us when these comforts are put out, but David's faith was comforted with this thought: he who blew out the candle can light up another. *Thou wilt light my candle: the Lord my God will enlighten my darkness.* Our faith may be comforted by this as well. The Lord will renew my comforts, alter the present sad state I am in, and chase away that trouble and darkness that is on me now. Just beware of offending him at whose signal your lights and comforts come and go. Michal displeased the Lord; therefore, she *had no child unto the day of her death* (2 Samuel 6:23).

Hannah waited humbly on the Lord for the blessing of children, and the Lord remembered her. He enlightened her condition with that comfort when she was a despised lamp. There is no comfort you have lost that God cannot restore, even double, if he sees it suitable for you.

Consideration 13. But if he does not restore your comforts, consider that even though he denies you any more comforts of this kind, he has something far better to give you. Those earthly comforts are not even worthy to be named with what he will give.

There is an excellent relevant scripture in Isaiah: *For thus saith the* LORD *unto the eunuchs that keep my sabbaths, and choose the things that please me, and take hold of my covenant; even unto them will I give in mine house and within my walls a place and a name better than of sons and of daughters: I will give them an everlasting name, that shall not be cut off* (Isaiah 56:4-5).

Men's names are to be continued in their children, in their male children especially. It was considered a loss of honor to not have sons (Numbers 27:4), and having numerous children was deemed a great honor (Psalm 127:4-5). So in the passage in Isaiah, God promised to supply and make good the lack of children and whatever honor here or memorial later they might have gained from having children by giving them something of far greater honor and something more enduring – a name better than and above the name of sons or daughters.

It is a greater honor to be the child of God than to have the greatest honor or comfort that children ever provided their parents in this world.

Dear heart, you are now dejected by this affliction that lies on you, as if all joy and comfort in this world are now cut off from you.

A cloud sits on all other comforts; this affliction has so embittered your soul that you taste no more in any other earthly comforts than in the white of an egg. Oh, if you would just consider the consolations that are with God for those who cooperate with his purpose in affliction, and patiently wait on him for their comfort! He has comforts for you far transcending the joy of children.

Some have discovered this when their children were cut off from them and to such a degree that they valued little their comfort in children in comparison with this comfort. I will give a meaningful example of this recorded by Robert Fleming, the worthy author of the book titled *The Fulfilling of the Scripture*:

One Patrick Mackewrath, who lived in the western parts of Scotland, had his heart touched by the Lord in a remarkable way. After his conversion (as he showed to many Christian friends), he was in such a state, so affected with the new world he had entered, the discoveries of God, and a life to come, that for some months he rarely slept because he was still filled with astonishment. His tenderness and close conversation with God in his walk were remarkable. What is worthy to be noted is that one day, after the sharp trial of having his only son suddenly taken away by death, he retired alone for several hours. When he came out from where he had been, he looked so cheerful that those around him asked the reason and wondered how he could be happy at a time like this. He told them that he had gotten that cheerfulness in his solitude with the

Lord, and if he could have it later renewed, he would be content to lose a son every day.

Oh, what a sweet exchange had he made! He gained gold in exchange for brass, a pearl for a pebble, a treasure for a trifle. So great and far greater is the disproportion between the sweet light of God's face and the faint, dim light of the best human joy.

I hope it will please the Lord to make this sun rise and shine on you now when the stars that shone with a dim and borrowed light have gone down. I hope you will see such gain by the exchange that you would quickly cast your vote with him we just mentioned and say, "Lord, let every day be like this funeral day; let all my hours be like this so that I may see and taste what I do now." How gladly I would part with the dearest and nearest creature comforts I own in this world. The gracious and tender Lord has his divine refreshing and healing drinks reserved for such sad hours. Sometimes these are given before a sharp trial to prepare us for it, and sometimes they are given after the trial to support us while under it.

I often heard a story from the mouth of a sweet Christian woman now with God, and later I found it in her diary. For several days and nights before the Lord removed her dear husband by death, there was such an abundant outlet of the love of God to her soul, that when the Lord took her husband in death, even though he was a gracious, sweet-tempered, and most tenderly loved husband, she was barely aware of the stroke of God. She was carried quite above all earthly things, their comforts, and their troubles, so that she almost lost the thoughts of her dear husband in God. She concluded that if the Lord had not done that for her, if he had not prepared her in that way, then the blow would have been too much for her, and she would have sunk beneath it.

A husband, a wife, a child are great, very great things, compared to other creatures, but certainly, they will seem like little things, next to nothing, when the Lord sets himself by them before the soul. How do you know that God has not called these earthly comforts aside this day to make way for heavenly ones? It may be that God is coming to communicate himself more sweetly, more perceptibly than ever to your souls, and these are the providences which must come and prepare the way of the Lord. Possibly God's meaning in their death is just this: "Child, stand aside. You are in my way and you take my place in your parent's heart."

Consideration 14. Be careful you do not excessively mourn in your grief for the loss of earthly things; consider that Satan takes advantage of all extremes.

In any extreme you experience, you will be touched by that Enemy whose greatest advantages lie in assaulting you here. Satan is called the ruler of the darkness of this world (Ephesians 6:12). That is, his kingdom is supported by darkness. There is a twofold darkness and this gives Satan great advantage. There is the darkness of the mind, namely, ignorance, and there is the darkness of the condition, the trouble and affliction. In the text, the apostle is speaking mainly of the darkness of ignorance, but Satan also often adds to our troubles to better carry out his designs on us. A dark hour of trouble with us is his best time to tempt us. That cowardly spirit falls on the people of God when they are down and low in spirit as well as in state. Satan would never have desired that the hand of God would have been stretched out on Job's person, estate, and children except that he promised himself a notable advantage in that situation to poison Job's spirit with vile thoughts of God. Do this, Satan said to God, and Job *will curse thee to thy face* (Job 1:11).

What the psalmist observes of natural darkness is also true of metaphorical darkness: *Thou makest darkness, and it is night: wherein all the beasts of the forest do creep forth. The young lions roar after their prey* (Psalm 104:20-21).

When it is the dark of night with men, it is noonday with Satan. Our time of suffering is his busiest time of work. He plants and grafts many dismal suggestions on our affliction, and these are much more dangerous to us than the affliction itself.

Sometimes he injects despairing thoughts into the afflicted soul: *For I said in my haste, I am cut off from before thine eyes* (Psalm 31:22). *My hope is perished from the* LORD: *remembering mine affliction and my misery, the wormwood and the gall* (Lamentations 3:18-19).

Sometimes he suggests harsh thoughts of God: *The Almighty hath dealt very bitterly with me* (Ruth 1:20). Yes, and he has dealt more severely with us than any other: *Behold, and see if there be any sorrow like unto my sorrow, which is done unto me, wherewith the LORD hath afflicted me in the day of his fierce anger* (Lamentations 1:12).

Sometimes Satan suggests thoughts of complaint and discontent against the Lord, and the soul is displeased at the hand of God on it. Jonah was angry at the hand of God and said, *I do well to be angry, even unto death* (Jonah 4:9). What dismal thoughts these are and much more distressing to a gracious soul than the loss of any outward enjoyment in this world.

Sometimes he suggests very irreverent and godless thoughts, as if there were no privilege to be had by Christianity, and all our pains, zeal, and care about duty were just a waste of time: *Verily I have cleansed my heart in vain, and washed my hands in innocency. For all the day long have I been plagued, and chastened every morning* (Psalm 73:13-14).

By these things, Satan gets a big advantage on the afflicted Christian. Although these thoughts are Satan's burden and God will not impute them to the condemnation of his people, yet they rob the soul of peace, hinder it from duty, and make it act unpleasant under affliction, to the stumbling and hardening of others in their sin. Be careful to not *give place to the devil* (Ephesians 4:27) by your excess of sorrow, *for we are not ignorant of his devices* (2 Corinthians 2:11).

Consideration 15. If you have any regard for the honor of God and Christianity, do not give way to excessive sorrows because of affliction, or you will expose them to reproach.

If you slight your own honor, do not slight the honor of God and Christianity too. Pay attention to how you behave in a day of trouble because many eyes are on you. It is a true observation that the late author Matthew Mead has made:

What will the atheist and what will the profane scoffer say when they see this? So foolish and malicious they are, that if they just see you in affliction, they immediately and scornfully demand: "Where is your God?"

But what would they say if they hear you unbelievingly cry out, "Where is our God?" They will be ready to cry, "This is the religion they make such a boast of. You see how little it does for them in a day of extremity. They talk of promises, rich and precious promises, but where are they now? What purpose do they serve? They said they had a treasure in heaven. Why do they mourn so, then, if their riches are there?"[3]

Be very careful what you do before the world. They have eyes to see what you can do as well as ears to hear what you can say, and as long as your behavior under trouble is so much like their own, they will never think your principles are better than theirs. The carnal people of the world will be drawn to think that no matter what fine things your mouths said about God and heaven,

---

3   Matthew Mead (1629–1699) was an English author and minister of a large congregation in London.

your hearts were on the same things that theirs were, since your grief at their removal is as great as theirs.

They know by experience what a support it is to the heart to have an able, faithful friend to depend on or to have hopes of soon inheriting a great estate. They will never be persuaded that you have any such ground of comfort if they see you as discouraged and cast down as those who do not pretend to have such things. By this manner, the precepts of Christ to faithfulness and contentment in all conditions will come to be looked on, like those of the Stoics, only as brave words but impossible to be practiced. The whole of the gospel will be taken for an empty and unsubstantial idea since they that profess the greatest regard for it are not helped by it at all. What a shame it is that religion, in this case, makes no difference between a Christian and a heathen! Show the world that you differ from them in humility, meekness, contempt of the world, and heavenly-mindedness, and let these graces display themselves by your cheerful and patient conduct under all your grievances.

God has planted those excellent graces in your souls so that he might be glorified and that you would benefit by the exercise of them in tribulation. If these are suppressed and hidden, and nothing but the pride, passion, and unsubdued earthliness of your hearts are at work and displayed in the time of trouble – what a slur, what a wound you will give to the glorious name that you call on. And if your hearts are truly gracious, that will pierce you deeper than the affliction that occasioned it ever did. If you will not be careful and tender about your own peace and comfort, be careful about the name of God.

Consideration 16. Be quiet and hold your peace because you do not know how many mercies lie in the womb of this affliction.

Sometimes the benefits of a sharp, rousing affliction to the people of God are great, and all the people might have the benefits at all times if they were more careful to use them to their advantage. David thankfully acknowledges, *It is good for me that I have been afflicted* (Psalm 119:71). Certainly, there is as much good in them for you as there was for him if the Lord sanctifies them to the ends and uses that David's were sanctified to.

Such a stinging rod as this did not come before there was need of it, and possibly you saw the need of some awakening providence yourselves. But if not, the Lord did. He took up the rod to strike you only when his faithfulness and tender love to your souls called on him to correct you.

You now sit pensively under the rod, sadly lamenting and deploring the loss of some earthly comfort. Your heart is excessively burdened with sorrow, your eyes run down with tears at every mention and remembrance of your dear friend. Why, this alone may reveal the need you had of this rod. Does not all this sorrow at parting plainly tell how much your heart was set on and how firmly your heart was glued to this earthly comfort?

Now that you see that your affections were sunk much deeper into the creature than you were aware of, what should God do in this case? Should he allow you to cling to the creature more and more? Should he permit it to steal and exhaust your love and delight and steal away your heart from himself? This he could not do and still love you. The more agitated you are under this affliction, the more you needed it.

What if by this stroke the Lord will awaken your drowsy soul and bring you out of that pleasant but dangerous spiritual slumber you had fallen into while you had pillowed your head on this pleasant, physical human comfort? This is better for you than if he should say, "Sleep on. He is joined to idols. Leave him alone! He is departing from me, the fountain, to a broken cistern; let him go!" (Hosea 4:17).

> The more agitated you are under this affliction, the more you needed it.

Yes, what if by this stroke on one of the most pleasant things you had in this world, God will reveal to you, more perceptibly and effectually than ever, the vanity both of that relationship and of all earthly comforts so that from now on you never give your heart, your hope, your love, and your delight to any of them as you did before? Before, you could talk of the creature's vanity, but I question if you ever had so clear and convincing a sight of its vanity as you do this day. Is this not considerable mercy in your eyes?

Now, if God is weaning you from all empty opinions and vain expectations from this world, and your judgment of the creature is rectified, and your affections for all other joys on earth are moderated, is this nothing? Oh, without a doubt, it is a greater mercy to you than to have your friend alive again.

What if by this rod your wandering, gallivanting heart will be whipped home to God? What if you resume your neglected duties and restore your decayed communion with God? What if you recover a spiritual and heavenly attitude of heart? What will you say then?

Certainly, you will bless the merciful hand that removed the obstructions and adore the divine wisdom and goodness that, by such a means as this, restored you to himself. Now you can pray more constantly, more spiritually, and more affectionately than before. It is a blessed rod that buds and blossoms with such fruits as these! Let this be marked as one of your best mercies, for you will have cause to eternally adore and bless God for this beneficial affliction.

Consideration 17. Do not allow yourselves to be overwhelmed by agitation and swallowed up in grief because God has tested you under a stinging rod. For even as stinging as it is, it is comparatively gentle to what others, even those as good as yourselves, have felt.

Your loved one is dead, but it is a single death. Others have seen the deaths of many of their loved ones at the same time. Your affliction is nothing compared to theirs. Zedekiah saw all his children murdered before his eyes and then had those eyes, too late, put out. The author of the book mentioned before tells us of a fine and godly gentlewoman in the north of Ireland who, when the rebellion broke out there, fled with three children, one of them still on the breast. They had not gone far before they were stripped naked by the Irish who, to their credit, spared their lives (it is likely, however, that they thought that cold and hunger would kill them). Afterward, going on at the foot of a river that runs to Lough Neagh, others encountered the family and intended to throw them into the river. But this godly woman was not dismayed and asked for a little liberty to pray. As she lay naked on the frozen ground, she resolved to not go to so unjust a death on her own feet. When she was called, she refused to come, so she was dragged by the heels along that rugged way to be thrown in the river with her little ones and company.

But then she turned and on her knees said, "You, I am sure, are Christians, and I can see you are men. In taking away our miserable lives, you do us a pleasure; but know that, as we never wronged you nor yours, you must remember you yourselves will die also and one day give an account of this cruelty to the Judge of heaven and earth." Hearing this, they resolved not to murder them with their own hands but instead put them on a small island in the river to die, naked and without any provisions.

The next day, the two boys, having looked around, found the hide of a beast that had been killed. The mother threw it over them while they were lying on the snow. The next day a little boat went by. She called out and asked them, for God's sake, to take them in, but they, being Irish, refused. She begged for a little bread, but they said they had none. Then she begged for a coal of fire. They gave that to her, and she made a little fire. The children took a piece of the hide, laid it on the coals, and then began to gnaw the leather, but without extraordinary divine support, what could this do?

They lived like this, without any visible means of help, for ten days. Their only bread was ice and snow, and their drink was water. Because the two boys were nearly starved, the woman asked them to go out of her sight so she did not have to watch their deaths; but God, at last, delivered them as miraculously as he had supported them all that while.

Judge whether a natural death, in an ordinary way, is comparable to such a trial as this, and yet the Lord did this to this godly and eminently gracious woman.

In his book, *None But Christ,* Mr. John Wall relates a sad story of a poor family in Germany who was driven into that condition by a famine. At last, the parents made a motion one to the other to sell one of the children so they could buy bread to sustain themselves and the rest. But when they came to choose which child to sell, their hearts so weakened, and they were so filled with compassion for every one of them, that they resolved instead to all die together. We read in Lamentations 4:10: *The hands of the pitiful women have sodden [cooked] their own children.*

Why do I speak of these extremities? How many parents, yes, some godly ones too, have lived to see their children dying in sin and profanity, and some by the hand of justice, lamenting their rebellion with a rope around their necks?

We know so little of the stings in the afflictions of others! Certainly, you have no reason to think the Lord has dealt more bitterly with you than others. It was a gentle stroke, a merciful act of Providence, if you compare it with what others have felt.

Consideration 18. If God is your God, you really have lost nothing by the removal of any creature comfort.

God is the fountain of all true comfort; creatures, the very best and sweetest, are just cisterns to receive and convey to us what comfort God is pleased to communicate. If the cistern is broken or the pipe is cut off so that no more comfort can be conveyed to us that way, he has other ways and means to do it, ways that we cannot even imagine. And if he pleases, he can convey his comforts to his people without any of them. And if God does it immediately, we will not be losers by that, for there are no comforts in the world that are so delectable and ravishingly sweet as those that flow directly from the fountain.

It is the sensuality of our hearts that causes us to feel for them so inordinately and grieve for the loss of them so excessively, as if we do not have enough in God without these human supplements.

The fullness of the fountain is yours, but you cast yourselves down because the broken cistern is removed. The best creatures are no better; Jeremiah spoke of God's people doing the same thing (Jeremiah 2:13). Cisterns have only what they receive, and broken ones cannot hold what is put into them. Why, then, do you mourn as if your life were bound up in the creature? You have as free access to the fountain as you had before. Heathens advise, and let them take comfort in it, that we repair, by a new earthly comfort, what we have lost in a former comfort. Seneca says, "You have carried to the grave him whom you loved. Seek one whom you may love in his place. It is better to repair than to mourn your loss." But if God never repairs your loss in things of the same kind, you know he can abundantly repair it himself.

Christian, is not one kiss of his mouth, one glimpse of his face, one seal of his Spirit a more sweet and substantial comfort than the sweetest relationship in this world can offer you? If the stream fails, then flee to the fountain; there is enough. God is where he was and what he was, even though the creature is not.

Consideration 19. Though you may lack a little comfort in your life, you will be rewarded with an easier death.

The removal of your friends before you may turn to your great advantage when your time is come to follow them. So many good souls have been choked and ensnared in their dying hour by the loves, cares, and fears they have had about those they must leave behind them in a sinful, evil world!

Your love for them might have proved a snare to you and caused you to be reluctant to go, hating to leave here. These are the things that make men loath to die. So might it have been with you unless God had removed your friends beforehand or gives you sights of heaven and tastes of divine love that will master and subdue all your earthly affections for these things.

I knew a gracious person, now in heaven, who, for

many weeks in her last sickness, complained that she found it hard to part with a dear relative, and that there was nothing that was a greater impediment to her soul than this. It is much easier to think of going to our friends who are in heaven before us than of parting with them and leaving our desirable and dear ones behind.

There are many cares and distracting thoughts you may then be pestered and distraught with on their account. "What will happen to them when I am gone? I am now to leave them to God only knows what wants, miseries, temptations, and afflictions in the midst of a deceitful, defiling, and dangerous world."

I know it is our duty to leave our fatherless children and friendless relatives with God, to trust them with him who gave them to us, and some have been enabled to do so cheerfully when they were parting from them. Luther could say, "Lord, you have given me a wife and children, I have little to leave them. Nourish, teach, and keep them, O Father of the fatherless and Judge of the widow." But not every Christian has Luther's faith. Some find it very hard to disentangle their affections at such a time. But if God has sent all yours ahead before you, you have so much less to do. Death may be easier for you than for others.

Consideration 20. If nothing I have said so far will persuade you, then lastly, remember that you are near that state and place that allows no sorrows for or sad reflections on any comforts like these.

In just a little while, you will not miss your loved ones and you will not need them. You will live as the angels of God. We now live partly by faith and partly by sense, partly on God and partly on the creature. We are in a mixed state; therefore, our comforts are too. But when God will be all in all and we will be as the angels of God in the way and manner of our living, life will be so different for us then from how it is now!

Angels neither marry nor are given in marriage, and neither will the children of the resurrection (Matthew 22:30). When the days of our sinning are ended, the days of our mourning will be too. No graves were dug until sin entered, and none will be dug after sin is banished.

Our glorified relatives will live with us forever. They will complain no more and die no more! This is the happiness of that state to which you are going. Your souls will be in the nearest union with God, the fountain of joy, and you will have no concerns apart from him. You will no longer have your patience tried or be subjected to such sorrows as you now feel. In just a little while, the end of all these things will come. Therefore, persevere as people who expect such a day of jubilee at any time.

> No graves were dug until sin entered, and none will be dug after sin is banished.

And with this, I have finished this section of this discourse, which was an attempt to dissuade you from the sin of excessive sorrow.

Chapter 4

Excuses

I will now proceed to remove the justifications and excuses for this excessive grief. It is natural for people, even good people, to justify their excesses, or at least try to diminish their seriousness, by making excuses for their emotions as if they did not have cause and reason enough to excuse them. If these pleas and excuses are fully addressed and answered, and the soul is convinced and left without apology for its sin, then the soul will be open to the means of its cure, which will be the final thing I address in this treatise.

My present task, then, is to satisfy those objections and answer those reasons which are commonly used to justify our excessive grief for lost loved ones. Though I will specifically talk about the relationship that the text directs, it applies to all other relationships as well.

Excuse 1. "You give me many reasons to meekly and quietly submit under this heavy stroke of God, but you know very little what stings my soul feels. The child was a child of many prayers. It was a Samuel begged of the Lord, so I concluded when I had it, that it brought with it the returns and answers of many prayers. But now I see it was nothing of the sort. God had no regard for my prayer about it, nor did he give it to me in that special way of mercy as I imagined it. Not only is my child dead, but in the same day, my prayers are shut out and denied."

Answer 1. It was your duty to pray for your children before you had them. If you did not pray for them submissively, and attribute to the pleasure of God the right to give or deny them, to keep them on earth or remove them as it seems good to him, then that was your sin. You are not to limit the Holy One of Israel, nor advise him, nor negotiate with him for what length of time you will enjoy your outward comforts. If you did so, it was your evil, and God has justly rebuked it by this stroke.

If you prayed submissively, attributing both the mercy asked and the continuance of it to the will of God, as you ought to do, then there is nothing in the death of your child that is in opposition to the true scope and intent of your prayer.

Answer 2. Your prayers may have been answered even though the thing prayed for is withheld, or if it was given, it was just for a little while and then taken away.

God answers prayers in four ways: he gives the thing prayed for immediately (Daniel 9:23), he suspends the answer for a time and then gives it (Luke 18:7), he withholds the mercy for which you ask and gives you a better one in its place (Deuteronomy 3:24; 34:4-5), or he gives you the patience to bear the lack or loss of it (2 Corinthians 11:9).

Now if the Lord has taken away your relative or friend and, in their place, has given you a meek, quiet, and submissive heart to his will, you do not need to say that he has shut out your cry.

Excuse 2. "I have lost a lovely, pleasing, and most endearing child, one that was beautiful and sweet. Only a hard, stony heart would not dissolve into tears at the loss of one so desirable, so engaging as mine was. It is no ordinary loss!"

Answer 1. The more lovely and attractive your loved ones were, the better will be your patience and contentment with the will of God in their death. There will be more loveliness, more self-denial, more grace. If they had been a thousand times more endearingly sweet than they were, they were not too good to deny for God.

Therefore, if obedience to the will of God does indeed master natural emotions, so that you look on patience and contentment as much more beautiful than the sweetest and most desirable joy on earth, then you may be able to be a testimony of the truth and strength of grace. You testify that you can, like Abraham, part with a child whom you so dearly love in obedience to the will of your God, whom you love infinitely more.

Answer 2. Although it must be acknowledged that it is a good gift from the hand of God, the loveliness and beauty of our children and relatives is just a common gift and often becomes a snare. In its own nature, our appearance is a transitory, vanishing thing, and therefore, it is not a great aggravation of the loss as you profess.

It is a common, ordinary gift. Eliab, Adonijah, and Absalom were as handsome as any in their generation (1 Samuel 16:6-7; 1 Kings 1:6; 2 Samuel 14:25). It is not only common to the wicked and the godly but even also to the animals. To most who excel in beauty and loveliness, it becomes a temptation. The souls of some would have been more beautiful and lovely if their bodies had been less so. Besides, our appearance is but a flower that flourishes in its month and then fades, so this should not be considered an aggravation of your trouble.

Answer 3. If your relatives sleep in Jesus, they will appear ten thousand times more lovely in the morning of the resurrection than they ever were in the world. What is the most perfect, purest beauty of mortals compared to the incomparable beauty of the saints in the resurrection? *Then shall the righteous shine forth as the sun in the kingdom of their Father* (Matthew 13:43). In this hope, you part with them; therefore, act suitably to your hopes.

Excuse 3. "My child was nipped off by death in the very bud; I only saw, loved, and then parted. If I had enjoyed her longer and had time to draw out the sweetness of such a joy, I could have endured it more easily. But their months or years with me were so few, that the child only served to raise expectations that were quickly and, therefore, more sadly dashed."

Answer 1. Did your friend die young, or was the bond of any other relationship dissolved almost as soon as it was made? Do not let not this seem an intolerable load to you, for if you have reason to hope they died in Christ, then they lived long enough in this world. It is truly said that they have sailed long enough who have reached the harbor, they have fought long enough who have won the victory, they have run long enough who have touched the goal, and they have lived long enough on earth who have won heaven – no matter how few their days here may be.

> What can you see in this world except sin or sorrow? A quick passage through it to glory is a special privilege.

Answer 2. The sooner your relative died, the less sin they committed and the less sorrow they felt. What can you see in this world except sin or sorrow? A quick passage through it to glory is a special privilege. Certainly, the world is not so desirable a place that Christians should desire even an hour longer in it for themselves or their friends, than serves to fit them for a better place.

Answer 3. You imagine that the parting would have been easier if the joy had been longer, but that is a sentimental and groundless conjecture. The longer you had enjoyed them, the stronger the feelings would have been. A young and tender plant may be easily pulled up by a single hand, but when it has spread and fixed its roots many years in the earth, it will require many strong blows and a hard tug to root it up.

Feelings, like those underground roots, are fixed and strengthened by nothing more than familiarity and long possession. It is much easier parting now than it would be later, no matter what you think. However, this should satisfy you: God's time is the best time.

Excuse 4. "I have lost all in one. It was my only one. I have none left in its place to repair the break and make up the loss. If God had given me other children to take comfort in, the loss would not have been so great, but to lose all at one stroke is intolerable."

Answer 1. The Christian religion does not allow Christians the liberty of expressing the death of their dear relatives by so hard a word as *loss*. They are not lost; they are sent before you. It is a shameful thing for a Christian to be rebuked for such an unfitting expression by a heathen. It is enough to make us blush to read what a heathen said about this: "Never say you have lost anything," says Epictetus, "but that it is returned. Is your son dead?[4] He is only restored. Is your inheritance

---

4   Epictetus (50–135) was a Greek Stoic philosopher who taught philosophy in Rome for almost twenty-five years.

taken from you? It is also returned." Later he adds, "Let everything be as the gods would have it."

Answer 2. It is not a fitting expression to say you have lost all in one, except if that one is Christ, and he, once being yours, can never be lost. Undoubtedly, you mean you have lost all your comfort of that kind. But what if you have? There are much higher, more durable, and more precious comforts still remaining. If you have no more of the one kind, as long as you have better, you have reason to rejoice!

Answer 3. You are imitating the way of the world too much in this complaint. The only way they know how to remedy the loss of one comfort is by another of the same nature, and this one must be put in the departed one's place to fill the vacancy. But you have another way to fill your loss. You have a God to fill the place of any creature that leaves you. Certainly, this excuse would be more appropriate for someone whose portion is in this life than for one who professes that God is his all in all.

> You have a God to fill the place of any creature that leaves you.

Excuse 5. "Oh, my only one is not only taken away but there is also no expectation or probability of any more. I must now look on myself as a dry tree, never to take comfort in children again, which is a distressing thought."

Answer 1. Suppose what you say is true, that you have no hope or expectation of another child; but if you have a hope of better things than children, you have no reason to be cast down. Bless God for higher and better hopes than these.

In Isaiah 56:5 the Lord comforts those who have no expectations of sons or daughters with this: *Even unto them will I give in mine house and within my walls a place and a name better than of sons and daughters: I will give them an everlasting name, that shall not be cut off.* There are better mercies and higher hopes than those you mourn. Though your hopes of children or hopes from children are cut off, if your eternal hopes are secure and are of the kind that will not make you ashamed; you should not be dismayed.

Answer 2. If God will not have your comforts lie any longer in children, then resolve to place them in himself, and you will never find a reason to complain of loss in that exchange. You will find in God what can never be found in any creature. Just one hour's communion with him will give you something that the happiest parents never had from their children; you will exchange brass for gold and fleeting vanity for solid and abiding excellency.

Excuse 6. "The suddenness of the stroke is overwhelming. God gave little or no warning to prepare me for this trial. Death executed its commission as soon as it received and opened it. My dear husband, wife, or child was snatched unexpectedly out of my arms by a surprising stroke, and this makes my stroke heavier than one would expect."

Answer 1. That the death of your relative was so sudden and surprising was to a great extent your own fault. You ought to have lived in the daily sense of their emptiness and an expectation of your separation from them. You knew they are a dying comfort in its best condition, and it is not an astonishing thing to see something dead that you knew before to be dying. Besides, you heard the deaths ringing around you in other families. You frequently saw other parents, husbands, and wives carrying out their dead. These were all warnings given to you to prepare for similar trials. Certainly, then, it was your own confidence and heedlessness that made this affliction so surprising to you, and there is no one to blame but yourself.

Answer 2. There is much difference between the sudden death of infants and that of grown-up persons. The latter may have much work to do to prepare for death. They will have many actual sins to repent of, and evidences of their share in Christ to examine and clear in order to make a more comfortable death, so they may seek to avoid sudden death. But the case of infants, who do not exercise their reason, is far different. They have no such work to do but are purely passive. All that is done to order their salvation is done by God immediately. It all comes to one, whether their death is quick or slow.

Answer 3. You complain of the suddenness of the

stroke, but another person will be ready to say, "If my friend had died in that manner, my affliction would have been nothing compared to what it is now. I have seen many deaths all rolled into one. I saw the gradual approach of death on my dear relative. They felt every thread of death as it came toward them and they often cried with Job, *Wherefore is light given to him that is in misery, and life unto the bitter in soul; which long for death, but it cometh not; and dig for it more than for hid treasures; which rejoice exceedingly, and are glad, when they can find the grave?* (Job 3:20-22)."

What you call the sting of your affliction, others would have counted a favor and privilege. How many tender parents and other relatives who loved their friends as dearly as yourselves have been forced to their knees for no other reason than to beg the Lord to hasten the separation of death and to put an end to the sorrow, which to them was much greater than the sorrow for the dead?

Excuse 7. "You pressure me to moderate my sorrows, and I know I ought to, but you do not know my situation. There is a sting in this affliction that only I can feel, and oh, how intolerable it is now! I did not act soon enough to get the proper help in time to save my loved one's life, or I erred in how to use the means of care. I now see the mistake I made, and I cannot help but see that I contributed greatly to their death, which I now, too late, mourn.

"Oh, my negligence, my recklessness, my thoughtlessness! My conscience now strikes me for my foolishness and aggravates my burden beyond what is usually felt by others! If I had acted in time and listened to and followed the advice of the doctors and those who were able to help, I might now have a living husband, wife, or child. But now, not only am I deprived of them, but I am also apt to think I have deprived myself of them. Surely there is no sorrow like my sorrow."

Answer 1. Though it is evil to neglect and slight the means ordained by God for the recovery of health, it is just as evil to attribute too much to them or rely too much on them. The best methods and means in the world are weak and ineffective without God's aid and agreement, and they never have his assistance or agreement when his time has come. The fact that your friend died shows that God's time had fully come. So even if your friend had had the most excellent help and care that the world can offer, they would have been of no benefit at all. This consideration only applies in this case, where you see and know what the will of God is by the outcome. This cannot be pled while the outcome is still dubious and uncertain, as it usually is in times of sickness.

> The best methods and means in the world are weak and ineffective without God's aid and agreement.

Answer 2. You are unjustly charging and blaming yourself for that which is not really your fault or neglect. How far you are chargeable in this case will best appear by comparing the circumstances you are now in with those you were in when your relative was still sick and you were uncertain what was your duty and the best course to take.

Perhaps you had observed so many die while in the hands of physicians and so many recover without them, that you judged it safer for your friend to be without those means than to be endangered by them. Possibly various methods and courses were prescribed and advised, and you now see your error in choosing the riskier method and neglecting what was safer and more probable. Yet as long as that was not your understanding at the time, and you followed the best light you had to guide you then, it is most unjust to charge yourself for choosing the course that seemed best to you then, whether it was or not.

To be angry with yourself now for doing or omitting what was done or omitted according to your best discretion and judgment then, because you now see it in hindsight, is to be angry and troubled that you are a human, that you are not as God, who alone can foresee outcomes and events, and that you acted as all rational creatures are bound to do according to the light they have at the time and season of action.

Answer 3. To conclude, times of great affliction are ordinarily times of great temptation, and it is common then for Satan to charge us with more sins than we are guilty of and to make things to be sins that are not sins.

If you had knowingly and voluntarily neglected your duty to your relative, or if you had not spent money for their care and treatment and chose to let them die rather than part with your money, then the evil of sin would be mixed with your affliction, and your conscience may justly strike you for it as sin. But if you did not, which is the more common situation, and I presume is yours, then it is a false charge, and you should not aid the design of Satan in it.

Judge by the sorrow you now feel because of your friend. How dear was he to you, and if it could be done with money, what would you willingly give to ransom his life? Judge by this how groundless the charge is that Satan now draws up against you, and do not be so ready to yield to the truth of it.

Excuse 8. "But my troubles are of greater concern and more severe. My child or friend has passed into eternity, and I do not know how it is with his soul. If I were sure that my relative was with Christ, I would be quiet, but my fears of the contrary are overwhelming. Oh, it is terrible to think of the damnation of one so dear to me!"

Answer 1. Even if it is true what your excuse supposes, that you have real grounds to fear the eternal condition of your dear relative, it is still utterly unfitting for you, even in such a case, to dispute with or complain against the Lord.

I confess it is a sore and heavy trial and that there is no cause sadder and more depressing to the spirit of a gracious person. His death is just a trivial matter compared to this, but if you fear the Lord, I think his indisputable sovereignty over our relatives and his distinctive love and mercy to you should at least silence you in this matter.

God has indisputable sovereignty over them. *O man, who art thou that repliest against God?* (Romans 9:20). The apostle speaks about the matters of eternal election and condemnation. If the Lord will not be gracious to those who are so dear to us, is there any wrong done to them or us? Aaron's two sons were cut off in the act of sin by the Lord's immediate hand, yet *Aaron held his peace* (Leviticus 10:3). God plainly told Abraham that the covenant would not be established with Ishmael even though Abraham had so earnestly prayed, *O that Ishmael might live before thee!* (Genesis 17:18). Abraham knew that there was no salvation apart from the covenant, yet he sat down silent under the word of the Lord.

But if this does not quiet you, I think God's distinctive love and mercy to you should do it. You owe God so much because he has not thrown both root and branch into the fire! The Lord has given you good hope, through grace, that it will be well with you forever. Let this close your mouth and quiet your spirit even though you have grounds for this fear.

Answer 2. I also ask you to examine the grounds of your fear to discern if they may actually come from the strength of your feelings for your relatives or from the subtlety of Satan, whose plan here is to overwhelm and swallow you up in supposed, as well as just, grounds and causes. In two cases, your fear may probably proceed only from your own feelings or from Satan's temptation.

The first instance would be if your relative died young before they did anything to destroy your hopes. The other instance would be if the person was grown up and promising to some degree, but neither in life nor in death gave evidence of grace with the clearness that you desired.

For the case of infants in general, it is none of our concern to judge their condition. And for those who were born to covenanted parents, it is fitting for us to exercise charity toward them, because the Scripture speaks very favorably of them.

As for the more adult ones, who have escaped the pollutions of the world and showed awareness of sin and duty but never demonstrated what you desired they had, perhaps still in them, as in young Abijah, may be *found some good thing toward the* Lord which you never took notice of (1 Kings 14:13). Respect for your authority, bashfulness, modesty, having a reserved disposition, and many other things may hide from the observations of their parents those small and weak beginnings of grace that are in children. God might see in them what you never saw; he does not despise the day of small things (Zechariah 4:8-10).

However it is, it is now out of your reach; your concern is to turn the affliction to your own good rather than judge and determine your friend's condition, which belongs not to you but to God.

Excuse 9. "Oh, but I have sinned in this relationship,

and God has punished my sin by dissolving it." "Oh," says one, "my heart was too fixed on it. I even idolized it, that was my sin!" Someone else says, "I did not love them as I should have, at least not as spiritually as I ought to have. That was my sin. Now God is afflicting me for all the neglect and defects in our relationship."

Answer 1. No person is so thoroughly sanctified that they will not fail and fall short in many things pertaining to their relationships. The sins and corruption of the holiest people are revealed in this as much as in any other. It is a very common thing for our conscience to not only charge us with these failures, but also to aggravate them to the utmost when God has made the separation by death. This is usual and very common with people in your situation.

Answer 2. Even if we allow what your excuse supposes, that God afflicted you for your sin and removed that comfort from you that you idolized and loved too much, there is still no reason you should be so depressed by your affliction. All of this may be, and probably is, the fruit of his love for and the care of your soul. To comfort the afflicted, God tells them, *As many as I love, I rebuke and chasten* (Revelation 3:19). It is much better to have an idolized pleasure taken from you in mercy than to have God say of you as he did of Ephraim, *[He] is joined to idols: let him alone* (Hosea 4:17).

It is better that your Father settles with you now for your foolishness with the rod in his hand than to say, as he does to some, "Let them go on. I will not stop them or rebuke them for their sinful path, but I will settle accounts with them altogether in hell at the end."

Answer 3. As to what you now claim, that your neglect of duty flowed from a lack of love for your relative, your sorrow at parting may be evidence that your relative was rooted deeply in your love. But if your love was not so spiritual and pure as to love and enjoy them in God, that was undoubtedly your sin and is the sin of most Christians for which you and all others ought to be humbled.

Excuse 10. "God has blessed me with an estate and physical comforts in the world that I planned to leave to my offspring, but now I have no one to leave them to, nor do I have any comfort from it. In an hour, the purposes of my heart were broken off, and the comfort of all my other pleasures was blasted by this stroke. The efforts, pains, and cares of many years are destroyed."

Answer 1. How many are there in the world, even those of our own acquaintance, whom God has either denied or deprived of the comforts both of children and estates? If he has left you those physical comforts, you ought to acknowledge his goodness in that and not slight these because he has deprived you of the other.

Answer 2. Though your children are gone, God has many children left in the world whose spirits you may strengthen and revive with what he has given to you, and your charity to them will undoubtedly turn more profit than if you had left a large estate to your own posterity.

Certainly, we are not sent into this world to heap up great wealth for our children. If you have been too eager to do this, you may now read God's just rebuke of your folly. Bless God that you still have an opportunity to serve him supremely by your charity. If God denies you other executors, let your hands be your executors, to distribute to the necessity of the saints so that those ready to perish may bless you (Romans 12:13).

Excuse 11. "Oh, but the memory of my child's witty words and pretty actions is wounding."

Answer 1. This should lift up your hearts to God in praise and thankfulness that he gave you so desirable a child, rather than fill your heart with discontent at his hand in removing it. There are so many parents in the world whose children God has deprived of reason and understanding, so that they only differ from animals in external shape and figure. How many children show such corrupt and obstinate tempers that their parents expect little comfort from them?

Answer 2. These are just small matters and trivial things in themselves, but by these little things, Satan schemes to dishearten or exasperate your soul. Certainly, this should not be your concern at this time; you have greater things to be concerned about than the words and actions of children. Your concern is to search out God's ends in the affliction, to destroy the sin it is sent to rebuke, and to quiet your hearts in the will of God.

Excuse 12. Last, it is objected, "God hides his face from me in my affliction; it is dark within as well as without, and this makes my situation most deplorable. I am afflicted and deserted."

Answer 1. Though you presently lack comfort you can feel, you have reason to be thankful for the support of grace. Though the light of God's face is not shining on you, you will find the everlasting arms are underneath you. The care of God is still working for you when the consolations of God are taken away.

Answer 2. To have God hide his face in time of trouble is not a new or unusual thing. God's dearest saints, even his own Son, have experienced it. The Son of God, in the depths of both inner and outer affliction, when wave called to wave, did not feel the sweet, perceptible influences of comfort from God that had always filled his soul before. If even Christ cried in his extremity, *My God, my God, why hast thou forsaken me?* (Matthew 27:46), then certainly we do not need to wonder as if some strange thing had happened to us.

> Though the light of God's face is not shining on you, you will find the everlasting arms are underneath you.

Answer 3. Perhaps it is obstinate behavior under the rod that is provoking God to hide his face from you. Consider this because nothing is more probable than for this to be the cause of God's withdrawal from you. If you could, in meekness and quietness, receive that cup your Father has given you to drink, accept the punishment of your sins, and say, "Good is the word of the Lord. *It is the Lord: let him do what seemeth him good*" (1 Samuel 3:18), you would soon find your situation changed. But the comforting Spirit finds no delight or rest in a turbulent and tumultuous heart.

With this, I have answered the most considerable attempts to justify our excesses.

Chapter 5

The Cure

I now come to the last thing proposed, namely, the means of curing and preventing these sinful excesses of sorrow for the death of our dear relatives. Although much has been said already to dissuade you from this evil, and I have already elaborated beyond what I intended, I will add some further help and assistance toward the healing of this disorder by prescribing the following rules:

Rule 1. If you do not want to mourn excessively for the loss of human comforts, then take care that you do not excessively and inordinately set your delight and love on them while you enjoy them.

Strong affections make strong afflictions. The higher the tide, the lower the ebb. Our grief in the loss of these things is to the same degree as our delight in the pleasure. The apostle Peter knits these two graces – temperance, or self-control, and persevering patience – together

(2 Peter 1:6), and it is very visible how intemperance and impatience are inseparably linked in experience, even the experience of the best men. You read, *Now Israel loved Joseph more than all his children, because he was the son of his old age: and he made him a coat of many colours* (Genesis 37:3).

This was the darling. Jacob's heart was exceedingly set on Joseph. His very life was bound up in the life of the lad. Now, when the supposed death of the child was brought to him, how did he respond? *And Jacob rent his clothes, and put sackcloth upon his loins, and mourned for his son many days. And all his sons and all his daughters rose up to comfort him; but he refused to be comforted; and he said, For I will go down into the grave unto my son mourning. Thus his father wept for him* (Genesis 37:34-35).

Here, as in a looking glass, the effects of excessive love for a child are represented. Here you see what excessive love will do, even in a sanctified heart.

Oh, *let your moderation be known unto all men* in your delight and sorrows about earthly things (Philippians 4:5). Usually, the proportion of the one is subject to the other.

Rule 2. If you do not want to be overwhelmed with grief by the loss of your loved ones, be exact and careful in carrying out your duties to them while you have them.

The testimony of your conscience that confirms you worked to carry out all your duties to your loved ones while they were with you will prove an excellent alleviation of your sorrows for them when they are no longer yours. It is not so much the affliction alone as the guilt charged to us in times of affliction that makes our load so heavy.

What a terrible thing it is to have to look on our dead friends while our conscience is accusing and rebuking us for neglecting our duties and committing whatever sins in our relationships. Think how dreadful this will make the body of your dead friend look to you!

Your conscience, if not completely foolish or dead, will speak at that time, so if you want to ensure a comfortable parting at death and a comfortable meeting again at the judgment, be careful, punctual, and vigilant in all your relationship duties.

Rule 3. If you do not want to be overwhelmed with distress at the loss of dear relationships, turn to God under your troubles and pour out your sorrows by prayer into his open arms.

This will ease and put to rest your distress. Blessed be God for the ordinance of prayer! The saints are indebted to it at all times, but especially in sad and distressful times! It is some relief when, in distress, we can pour out our trouble into the heart of a wife or faithful friend. How much more when we leave our problems before the gracious, wise, and faithful God!

> Turn to God under your troubles and pour out your sorrows by prayer into his open arms.

I told you before of that holy man who, having lost his dear and only son, went to his prayer closet and there freely poured out his soul to the Lord. His friends, who feared how he would bear that stroke, were waiting down below to comfort him. But the man came down from his prayers with a cheerful countenance and told his friends he would be content to bury a son every day, if it were possible, provided he would enjoy the same comfort his soul had found in that private hour.

Christian, go to your God. Get to your knees in the cloudy and dark day. Go away from all other creatures so you may have full liberty with your God, and there, pour out your heart before him in free, full, and brokenhearted confessions of sin. Judge yourself worthy of hell as well as of this trouble. Justify God in all his stinging blows. In your distress, beg him to put out his everlasting arms. Plead for one smile, one gracious look from God to brighten your darkness and cheer your drooping spirit. Say with the prophet, *Be not a terror unto me: thou art my hope in the day of evil* (Jeremiah 17:17), and test to see what relief this will give you. If your heart is sincere in this, you will be able to say with that holy man, *In the multitude of my thoughts within me thy comforts delight my soul* (Psalm 94:19).

Rule 4. If you want to bear the loss of your dear relatives with moderation, then view God in the whole process of the affliction more, and secondary causes and circumstances of the matter less.

I was dumb, I opened not my mouth; because thou didst it (Psalm 39:9). Consider the hand of the Lord in the whole matter. Consider it first as a sovereign hand that has the right to dispose of you and all your comforts without your permission or consent (Job 33:13).

Second, consider it as a father's hand correcting you in love and faithfulness. *For whom the* LORD *loveth he correcteth; even as a father the son in whom he delighteth* (Proverbs 3:12). Oh, if just once you could see affliction as a rod in a father's hand, springing from his love and intended for your eternal good, how quiet you would be then! And if it draws your heart nearer to God and deadens it more to this vain world, it is a rod in the hand of special love. If your trial ends in your love for God, do not doubt that it comes from God's love for you.

> Consider God's hand as a moderate and merciful hand that has punished you less than your sins deserve.

Third, God's hand comes as a just and righteous hand. Did you not bring this affliction on yourself by your own foolishness? The Lord is just in all that has come upon you. Whatever he has done, he has done you no wrong.

Fourth, consider God's hand as a moderate and merciful hand that has punished you less than your sins deserve. He who has cast you into affliction might justly have cast you into hell. *It is of the* LORD's *mercies that we are not consumed* (Lamentations 3:22). *Wherefore doth a living man complain, a man for the punishment of his sins?* (Lamentations 3:39).

Rule 5. If you want to bear your affliction with moderation, compare it with the afflictions of other men, and that will greatly quiet your spirit.

You have no cause to say that God has dealt bitterly with you and that there is no sorrow like your sorrow. Look around you and impartially consider the condition that others are in. These are people who are not inferior to you in any way. You lost one dear child, but Aaron lost two at one stroke, and Job lost all. Both of these were by an immediate stroke from the hand of God. Some godly parents have lived to see their children die in their sin by the hand of justice, and others have seen them live to the dishonor of God and the breaking of their own hearts. They would have, along with Job, regarded it a mercy if they had died at birth (Job 3:11).

Some parents have watched their children die in such misery! They saw so much pain, misery, and suffering in their children, that they persistently begged the Lord to loose his hands and cut their children off. In their estimation, death was nothing compared to those continual agonies in which they have seen them lie writhing from day to day. You know so little what bitter cups others have been given to drink! If you compare, certainly you must say, "The Lord has dealt gently and graciously with me."

> Do not increase your sorrow by the sight of or conversations about sad subjects.

Rule 6. Carefully shun and avoid whatever might renew your sorrow or cause you to stop persevering.

Do not increase your sorrow by the sight of or conversations about sad subjects. Work to avoid them as occasions presented by the Enemy of your souls to pull out the sin of your heart.

I told you before that Jacob would not have Rachel's child called after the name his wife had given, Benoni, "the son of my sorrow." He did not want there to be a daily reminder that would renew his sorrow for the loss of his dear wife, so he called his name Benjamin.

Your restlessness is like kindling or gunpowder. As long as you can prevent sparks from falling on it, there is no great danger. But you who carry such dangerous matter in your own hearts need to be extra vigilant to prevent the sparks. Do with murmuring what you do with blasphemous thoughts – think a completely different way and do not give them a foothold.

Rule 7. In the day of your discontent for the death of your friends, seriously consider both that your own death is approaching and that you and your dead friend are separated by a small interval and point of time: *I shall go to him* (2 Samuel 12:23). The thoughts of your own approaching death will certainly still and quiet your sorrows for the dead that have gone before you.

We are prone to imagine a long life in the world, so then the loss of those comforts that we promised ourselves so much of the sweetness and joy of our lives from seems intolerable. But if you would realize your own death more, you would not be as deeply concerned about their death as you are. If you would look into your own grave more seriously, you would be able to look into your friend's grave more calmly.

I have now finished what I purposed. May the Father of mercies and God of all comfort, whose sole prerogative it is to comfort them who are cast down, write all his truths on your hearts. May these truths abide there and reduce your disordered and unbalanced emotions to the form that best suits the will of God and the profession you make of your subjection and resignation to his will.

John Flavel – A Brief Biography

"I could say much, though not enough of the excellency of his preaching; ... of his plain expositions of Scripture; his talking method, his genuine and natural deductions, his convincing arguments, his clear and powerful demonstrations, his heart-searching applications, and his comfortable supports to those that were afflicted in conscience. In short, that person must have a very soft head, or a very hard heart, or both, that could sit under his ministry unaffected."[5]

The parishioner who wrote this of his pastor, John Flavel, has been joined in his admiration by William Wilberforce, Jonathan Edwards, Increase Mather, and many others. Mather, an influential American Puritan and president of Harvard College, wrote, "[John Flavel's] works, already published, have made his name precious in both Englands; and it will be so, as long as the earth shall endure."[6]

John Flavel's life began sometime between 1627 and 1630 in Bromsgrove, Worcestershire, England. He was the older son of Richard Flavel, a Nonconformist minister, a pastor of a Protestant church not part of the Church of England. In his early years, he was educated at home and in the local grammar schools, and after doing well there, he was sent to study at University College in Oxford.[7]

In 1650, after earning his degree, Flavel was asked to be an assistant to the minister of Diptford in Devon, a county in the far southwest of England. The minister was an older man, and Flavel succeeded him at his death. It was here that he married the first of his four wives, Jane Randal. They were happily married until

---

[5] Anonymous, introduction to *The Whole Works of the Rev. Mr. John Flavel*, by John Flavel (London: W. Baynes and Son, 1820) 1:vi, http://www.digitalpuritan.net/Digital%20Puritan%20Resources/Flavel%2C%20John/The%20Whole%20Works%20of%20John%20Flavel%20%28vol.1%29.pdf

[6] Increase Mather, "To the Reader" in *An Exposition of the Assembly's Catechism* by John Flavel in *The Works of John Flavel* (London: Banner of Truth Trust, 1968, 6:139, quoted in Brian H. Cosby, *John Flavel: Puritan Life and Thought in Stuart England* (Lanham: Lexington Books, 2013), 13.

[7] Anonymous, *Whole Works*, 1:iv.

November of 1655 when Jane (and their son) died during childbirth. After a year of mourning, he married again to Elizabeth Stapell. It too was a happy marriage, and they were blessed with children.

After 6 years in Diptford, the people of Dartmouth called Flavel to be their pastor. Dartmouth was a great seaport and a much larger town. After praying and receiving the urging and blessing of his neighboring ministers, he accepted the call and moved to Dartmouth in late 1656. Here he was known for being well-read and a diligent learner (he knew at least eight languages), but he adapted his style and words to his less educated hearers who were mostly farmers and sailors. Flavel preached every Sunday and held popular Wednesday lectures. He was passionate in prayer, and "God crowned his labours with many conversions."[8]

The year 1662 marked the beginning of years of suffering for John Flavel and many others. Twenty years earlier, religious conflict had contributed to the start of the English civil war and the dismantling of the Anglican Church under Oliver Cromwell. Now with the return of the monarchy and Charles II, the Church of England was fully restored, a revised prayer book was approved, and the time of "The Great Persecution" began.[9] In 1662, Parliament passed the Act of Uniformity. This law, among other things, prescribed prayers, sacraments, and rites of the church according to the Book of Common Prayer. Almost 2,000 clergymen, including

---

[8] Anonymous, *Whole Works*, 1:vi.
[9] "Living Heritage: Persecution," UK Parliament, accessed July 17, 2021, http://www.parliament.uk/about/living-heritage/transformingsociety/private-lives/religion/overview/.

Flavel, refused to comply with this act and were expelled from the Church of England. The Conventicle Act of 1664 barred Nonconformists from holding separate church services, and the Five Mile Act of 1665, yet another law passed in an attempt to suppress dissent, prohibited expelled ministers from living in or even coming within 5 miles of any corporate town or a town where they had previously pastored. In 1665, Flavel's mother and father were arrested for participating in an illegal prayer meeting held in a private home. While imprisoned, his parents contracted the plague. They both became fatally ill and were released to die.

During these tumultuous times, Flavel stayed faithful to his congregation and his God. He had lost his living and had to move five miles away, but he continued to serve despite the threat of penalties and persecution. He preached in the woods at midnight, on an island in poor weather, and in fields of neighboring villages. Many times, he sneaked back to Dartmouth to preach and encourage his flock in private houses. He resorted at times to disguises and even riding his horse straight into the ocean to avoid capture from pursuing soldiers.[10] His second wife died during these years, and Flavel married a third time to Ann Downe, who gave birth to two sons. (Though it is not clear, it seems Flavel had three surviving children – two sons and a daughter.)[11]

In 1672 there was a brief reprieve when Charles II issued the Royal Declaration of Indulgence, which

---

10 Cosby, *John Flavel*, 18-19.
11 Nathan Parker, "Proselytisation and Apocalypticism in the British Atlantic World: The Theology of John Flavel" (PhD diss., Durham University, 2012), 17, fn.2, http://etheses.dur.ac.uk/7276/.

gave Nonconformists the freedom to worship, and Flavel returned to Dartmouth as a Congregationalist pastor. But that indulgence was canceled the next year, so Flavel returned to preaching in houses and fields – and writing.[12]

Puritan pastors had more time to write while they were forbidden to preach, and Flavel was no exception. He wrote mostly for his congregation; several books were addressed specifically to sailors and farmers. Many of his works were on suffering, a subject with which he was most familiar, but Flavel always wrote with the desire to make Christ known and for the conversion of souls.

While Mather's prediction about Flavel being revered as long as the earth will last was not realized, Flavel did leave a lasting legacy and "deeply influenced those who would set the course as shapers of church and culture in the generations to follow"[13] through his writings. His collected works went through at least thirteen editions during the eighteenth century alone, and his works have been printed hundreds of times.[14] Flavel was one of the best-selling authors in England and in the American colonies.[15]

Sometime in 1676-77, Flavel's third wife died. Flavel stayed in Dartmouth until 1682 when the danger drove him to London. Here he met and married his fourth

---

12 Joel Beeke, "John Flavel (1628-1691)," Banner of Truth, April 13, 2006, https://banneroftruth.org/us/resources/tag-index/.
13 Cosby, *John Flavel*, ix.
14 Brian Cosby, "The Works of John Flavel: A New Edition," *Reformation21*, August 15, 2018, https://www.reformation21.org/blogs/the-works-of-john-flavel-a-new.php.
15 Nathan Parker, "Proselytisation and Apocalypticism," 23-24, 256-258, 265-266.

wife, a widow named Dorothy Jeffries. He stayed in London for two years then returned to Dartmouth and ministry to his scattered congregation. By the time of the Glorious Revolution in late 1688, when James II was deposed and religious freedom granted to the Nonconformists, Flavel was nearing his end. He preached his last sermon while visiting Exeter on June 21 and died suddenly of a stroke on June 26, 1691. He was returned to Dartmouth and buried in the churchyard.

Other Similar Titles

Absolute Surrender, by Andrew Murray

God waits to bless us in a way beyond what we expect. *From the beginning, ear has not heard, neither has the eye seen, what God has prepared for those who wait for Him* (Isaiah 64:4). God has prepared unheard of things, things you never can think of, blessings much more wonderful than you can imagine and mightier than you can conceive. They are divine blessings. Oh, come at once and say, "I give myself absolutely to God, to His will, to do only what God wants." God will enable you to carry out the surrender necessary, if you come to Him with a sincere heart.

Available where books are sold.

Faithful to Christ,
by Charles H. Spurgeon

If there is a true faith, there must be a declaration of it. If you are a candle, and God has lit you, then l*et your light so shine before men that they may see your good works and glorify your Father who is in the heavens* (Matthew 5:16). Soldiers of Christ must, like soldiers of our nation, wear their uniforms; and if they are ashamed of their uniforms, they ought to be drummed out of the army.

Available where books are sold.

The School of Obedience,
by Andrew Murray

For us to have favor with God, obedience is of utmost importance. *To obey is better than sacrifice* (1 Samuel 15:22). This is evident from the very beginning of the Bible to the very end: *Blessed are they that do His commandments, that they may have a right to the tree of life* (Revelation 22:14).

Let this study awaken in you an earnest desire to fully know God's will concerning this truth. Let us unite in praying that the Holy Spirit will show us how defective the Christian's life is in which obedience does not rule everything. Let us desire to learn how that life can be exchanged for one of full surrender to absolute obedience, and how certain it is that God, through Christ, will enable us to live it out.

Available where books are sold.

The Power of Prayer and the Prayer of Power,
by Reuben A Torrey

Prayer is the key that unlocks all the storehouses of God's infinite grace and power. All that God is, and all that God has, is at the disposal of prayer; but we must use the key. Prayer can do anything that God can do, and since God can do anything, prayer is omnipotent. No one can stand against the person who knows how to pray, who meets all the conditions of prevailing prayer, and who really prays, and if they are willing to pay the price. The price is prayer, much prayer, much real prayer, prayer in the Holy Spirit.

Available where books are sold.

Morning by Morning,
by Charles H. Spurgeon

Charles H. Spurgeon's devotionals *Morning by Morning* and *Evening by Evening* have inspired, encouraged, and challenged Christians for generations. Spurgeon, with his masterful hand, carefully selected his text from throughout the Bible and covered a broad range of topics, in order to present a well-balanced and fruitful daily devotional for readers both young and old.

Now updated into more-modern English for today's readers, and again separated into two volumes as originally published, with morning devotionals in one volume and evening devotionals in the second. We chose a 11-point font for the sake of legibility, and formatted the devotionals so each fits on a single page.

Available where books are sold.

Life in Christ Vol 1,
by Charles H. Spurgeon

Men who were led by the hand or groped their way along the wall to reach Jesus were touched by his finger and went home without a guide, rejoicing that Jesus Christ had opened their eyes. Jesus is still able to perform such miracles. And, with the power of the Holy Spirit, his Word will be expounded and we'll watch for the signs to follow, expecting to see them at once. Why shouldn't those who read this be blessed with the light of heaven? This is my heart's inmost desire.

Available where books are sold.

www.ingramcontent.com/pod-product-compliance
Lightning Source LLC
Chambersburg PA
CBHW070145080526
44586CB00015B/1848